Imani Faith Publishing Presents

NO TEST NO TESTIMONY EVIDENCE OF GOD'S FAITHFULNESS

Compiled by

Award Winning Author Best – Selling Author

Cheryl Lacey Donovan

DEDICATION

This book has truly been a labor of love for everyone involved. It is never easy to relive the painful experiences in your life. Yet, each of these ladies chose, without hesitation, to share their testimonies so that other women might be saved from themselves.

We dedicate this book to every woman regardless of race, creed, color, or socio-economic status because we know that the issues addressed in this book are no respecter of person. We pray that those who read through these pages will find themselves and be set free from their bondage.

ACKNOWLEDGEMENTS

I'd like to first of all acknowledge my God. He is my sustainer, my deliverer, my savior, and my friend. As I grow more mature in Him, I see His divine hand in every aspect of my life. I thank Him vehemently for this full circle moment where I can help others to tell their stories just as Peace in the Storm Publishing has helped me.

Therefore, my next acknowledgment goes to my sister friend, my colleague, my partner, and my mentee in many ways. Thank you for allowing me to carry a part of your legacy (Peace in the Storm Publishing) by allowing me to publish books through the Imani Faith Publishing imprint. It is truly an honor to give to others what you gave to me so many years ago; a chance to have a voice.

To my family, most specifically my husband, thank you for loving me, for believing in me and for being the priest, provider and protector of our home. Mama, thank you for instilling in me that never say die spirit that keeps me going and going and going.

Lastly, to the ladies who had the courage to tell their stories in the pages of this book, Shamarian, Denika, Olevia, Clara, Ramona, Letisha, Cee Cee, Nicolette, and Esther, thank you for trusting me with your words, your stories- your testimonies. Thank you for being willing to share this with the world.

We are overcomers by the word of our testimonies.

Where faith without works is dead

ISBN-13: 978-0692571811
ISBN-10: 0692571817

Library of Congress Control Number: 2015918654

IMANI FAITH PUBLISHING, LLC
A Division of Peace in the Storm Publishing, LLC
11601 Shadow Creek Parkway Ste. 126 Pearland, Texas 77548

Visit our Website at: www.imanifaithpublishing.com

TABLE OF CONTENTS

Table of Contents

Commentary by Cheryl Lacey Donovan

INTRODUCTION

Cheryl Lacey Donovan

Drug addiction, prostitution, domestic violence, child abuse, bullying, unforgiveness and shame sounds like the makings of a great urban fiction novel. But wait a minute, these are true stories. Stories of ridicule, retribution, and finally redemption. *No Test No Testimony* is a no holds barred look at the lives of ten women who have experienced some of the most tumultuous storms life has to offer. Yet, they have managed to find peace in the storm. You'll laugh, you'll cry, but most importantly you'll be transformed as you identify your truth between the pages of this book.

Imani Faith Publishing presents *No Test No Testimony*, riveting, heart-wrenching testimonies of triumph that give you evidence of God's faithfulness from some of the most prolific overcomers of our time.

LOST CHILD

Olevia Henderson

What can I say? In life there are lessons we all learn. Mine was not to trust my parents as I was growing up. Because my mother was an alcoholic and an abuser, the court felt it would be better for me to live with my Dad. My Father had been out of my life for as long as I could remember. Nevertheless, it was a dream come true to be moving in with Him. He was a single Dad and would now be raising five children on his own. In my mind it was all fun. He had moved off "the hill" in Allendale, the rear of Alston, to Logan Street. At first he was nice; or so it appeared. See, I soon discovered my life with him would riddled with abuse just as it had been with my mother. The only difference, it wasn't sexual. When reality hit there was no denying my father was what I learned to call a functioning alcoholic. He would get drunk every day and double on the weekend. Yet, he was still able to get up at daybreak, go to work, and work all day without a drink. But at quitting time, he would go in his cooler in his car and start drinking Miller's beer.

When I arrived at my new home my oldest sister Tamara asked, "Why did you come to stay with him? You should have stayed with your mama because he is going to beat you!"

I looked at her and asked, "Why you say that?"

She said, "Because that is all he does to us."

Still I was excited to stay. It wasn't until the first time I saw him beat my brothers and sisters that I began to have second thoughts. My dad was very strict. We could not go outside with the other kids. And as girls, if we did, we had better keep our gaze straight ahead. We could not even have the appearance of looking a little boys' way or we would have hell to pay.

Still because we were children we found ways to associate ourselves with the neighborhood children. When my dad went to work they would come to our back door so we could talk to them. In fact, my sister had a crush on one of the boys. His name was Richard. I on the other hand liked his cousin Reginald. Needless to say, the first beating I got from my dad was because of Reginald. I will never forget that day. I was an asthmatic. On this particular day the attack I had was severe so I had to stay inside. As usual we started letting the kids in our house to play. When Reginald arrived at the back door he asked my sister Tamara, "Where is Olevia?"

"Olevia is sick," she replied.

"Can I come in," he said

Tamara stepped back and allowed Reginald to enter the house. I was laying in the bed so he sat at the bottom and we started talking. What we didn't know was our neighbor Mr. Moore was telling our dad about all the fun we were having while he was away at work. Being aware of the situation, my dad parked his car away from the house this day and walked home. He came in and saw Reginald. Immediately the fear set in. He asked him, "Boy how you got in my house?"

Reginald replied "Through the front door!"

My dad asked, "Who let you in?"

He said, Tamara."

My dad then asked smugly, "How you think you getting out?"

Reginald said curtly, "through the front door!" He got up and walked out.

My dad was so mad that he got the extension cord and started swinging. He didn't care where he hit me. Then he started beating my sister. He didn't stop.

When the holidays finally arrived we were so happy. So, we decided we would cook a cake. My father got so mad he threw the cake in the sink and ran water on it. It goes without saying we got beat for that. We were told we were to cook dressing first. Because we didn't know how we called our grandma and asked her how to cook dressing so we wouldn't get another whooping.

Around 2am we figured we would be in the clear but we weren't. He was still fussing at us. His rants had now turned to the amount of money he was spending on Tamara and I. His solution was for us to get out of his house and in his words "Go make his rent money". We were crying and I was scared. He said, you better not come back without the money."

Tamara asked, "How are we supposed to get the money?"

He said, "You can walk the street for all I care but you better have it."

I refused to leave. I said, "I would rather get beat but I'm not going out in the streets."

Tamara told me to come with her but I refused. I begged her not to go. As she was leaving my dad asked, "Where you going?"

Indignantly Tamara said, I don't know but I will get the money." Then she left.

He didn't go to look for her until the next day. My sister was gone. She had managed to contact her mom in Houston who wired her a greyhound bus ticket. When dad went to work we walked our sister to the bus station. We later called and told him we woke up and she was gone. I asked myself and God why I was constantly being punished.

My dad was a ticking time bomb. With my oldest sister gone, I was now the one in charge of looking after my younger siblings. I cooked, I cleaned and I made sure everything was ok. A lot for someone that young. I was hurt and I was scared.

Dad's rules not only applied at home. They also followed us to the schoolhouse. He warned us that no one was to use our lockers. Well unfortunately I allowed a classmate to put her stuff in my locker. He popped up at Hamilton Terrace School and wanted to check my locker. When he say her books and shoes he threw them in the trash. During his search and seizure he noticed I had make up on. I denied it but he rubbed his hands across my eye and saw the black markings of the eyeliner on his fingers. He checked me out of school so I knew I was in trouble. I had to give him the eyeliner pencil. He then pulled his knife out and commenced to peel the wood from around it. Once he was done made me eat the eyeliner. I had to roll it in paper in order to chew it and swallow it. Shortly thereafter he took a marker and drew two lines under my eyes and made me sit outside so the kids could see. My two brothers laughed and made fun of not only the markings under my eyes but also our dresses. Infuriated my dad made them put the dresses on and sit outside next to me. I hated him and I hate the fact I told the judge I wanted to stay with him. Ironically, even though his intention for having us outside was embarrassment we were children, we were just happy to be outside.

Except for his girlfriend's house my father would take us everywhere he went. Because he would drink and pass out my siblings and I learned to drive at early ages. Me at 13, my sister Shasha at 11 and my brothers at 8 and 9. We was forced to grow up before our time. If he went to the club he would park his car in the front of the club with us in the car while he went in to party.

Our lives continued to be filled with abuse. Beatings were commonplace for us. By now my dad had pad locked the kitchen door and gave us one cup. He told us if we wanted water we would have to get it from the bathroom. We only ate when he would come home. It didn't matter the time. Grits and eggs or beans and cornbread was what he fed us. He on the other hand ate well. Especially when he made visits to his girlfriend's house. Minnie was her name. At least that is who he was with while I was there.

It became very apparent that life for Minnie wasn't much better with him than it was for us. There was a time I thought he was going to kill her. She had broken up with him. He of course didn't like that. He went to her home and forced her and her daughter in the car. He brought her to our house and he told us to watch her daughter. He had taken the rod out of the closet you -know the one that holds the clothes. He beat her so bad that when he hit her in the top of her head I saw a piece of her hair and scalp get knocked out of her head. When she fell he continued to beat her as she screamed for her life. We watched him beat her repeatedly with that rod. Her daughter was screaming and crying as well so he hit her in her face with the stick until her eyes were black and swollen. He refused to let her leave. He made her stay and watch in agony; helpless to do anything about it. I remember asking her was she ok when he left to go to the store to get more beer. We both just sat there crying. I just wanted to be away from him. The dad I wished for was not what I got. Minnie never came back after being held there for days. I wished I had left like my sister.

Shasha and I had an appointment to get our hair done. I had forgotten my house key so I stopped at their elementary school and got their key. As I walked down the alley I saw our screen off the kitchen window. I thought nothing of it so I walked to the front of the house and upon entering in the house and going to my dad's room I saw the television gone and the room was in a mess and papers thrown everywhere.

I looked at the backdoor in the kitchen. It was still locked and the board was across it. I quietly backed out of the house ran to get Mr. Moore to come go back in the house with me. He refused. I then ran to the next door neighbor and told her and she got her gun and came with me. When we walked in the back door was now wide open!!! Someone was in the house when I had entered it from school. Whoever it was managed to leave before I came back. I put all the stuff back in place and since the television had not been taken, it was left on the kitchen counter, I put it back. When my sister and brothers got home and I told them what happened they were glad nothing was taken. We got our hair done.

Once my dad made it home Mr. Moore told my dad about the break in. He rushed to the beauty shop. We had not started getting our hair done so he grabbed me up in the beauty shop and began yelling and screaming. "What boy broke in my house?"

"I don't know who broke in." I said

"You lying," he screamed.

He drove us back home. I was still in my Booker T Washington High school P.E uniform as he drug me in the house by my hair and made me show him where the TV was in the kitchen. He took his belt off and started beating me. I was screaming and yelling for him to stop. He told me he was beating me until I told him who broke in. At that moment he took his car keys and put a key between each finger and made a fist like brass knuckles. He punched me in the face so hard I landed against the washing machine. With blood pouring out of my nose I couldn't breathe. Instantly I knew my nose was broken. I could feel my eyes swelling up. I stood back up and he said, "Oh you gonna bleed on my floor?"

I said, "No sir." I was trying to catch the blood before it hit the floor.

Then he said, "So now you gonna let it get on the P.E. clothes I just bought?"

I was crying trying to stop the blood from getting anywhere holding my hands over my nose. He told me I thought I was too pretty especially with that long hair. He said he was gonna cut my hair. We only had one pair of scissors in our house they were sewing shears with ridges. As he went to the front of the house to get them I ran out the back door. I ran to an empty house and hid. I saw him flying down the alley looking for me in the car. Once he turned left down the alley, I ran from that house. I ran hard and fast. Somehow I managed to make it to a cousin's house in Lakeside. They helped me get to Cedar Grove to my aunt's house. She called the police. They came and took me to the hospital where they reset my broken nose. I was placed in foster care after they questioned my dad. He told them he didn't hit me. The story he concocted was that I fell and hit my face on the edge of the washer. Ironically, he wasn't arrested. CPS was called and I was placed in the custody of the state. I told them everything that went on in our home; about all the abuse. I told them they had to talk to my younger sister and brothers at school. Once they did, they were removed from the home as well. I felt free and safe no more beatings.

Being in foster care was almost as scary as being with my mother and father. I will never forget how my first foster mother abused her kids. I ran away from her. I was soon placed with another lady that I grew to love as if she was my grandmother. But my dad found out where I was and tried to come to see me.

However, Big Momma, as I called her wouldn't let him and I was glad. After that I only got to see my sister and brother once. It was during a visit with our dad. He was so busy telling me it was my fault that all this happened that I told my case worker I didn't want to go back to anymore visits. I didn't.

Through the court process I was given back to my mother. I can remember thinking the entire time how come I couldn't have a dad that loves me. Why did he beat me; beat us? It is a sad feeling when the people you trust and love fail to protect you.

It is amazing how life comes full circle. As I got older and I started having kids and eventually found my way back to my dad. He would apologize to me and acknowledge he was wrong. He would say he loved me. I never got that from my mother.

I know what made me forgive my father is that he admitted he was wrong. He asked me to forgive him and he allowed me to express my feelings. Often we go through life with the wounds buried inside never talking about them again. I learned "Not all wounds gush blood." No one has a right to harbor un-forgiveness. Jesus Christ was pure, sinless, without any shadow of deceit and he died on the cross to forgive us. So I learned I had no right to deny forgiveness to another person. We are all sinners in need of forgiveness and salvation.

I've found that when we are in a place where we can sit down and talk to the person that hurt us it helps us heal. My dad heard me out and I respectfully listened to him. He was a single dad raising 5 kids alone. He didn't have a good job and was barely making any money. He was stressed and didn't know the proper way to discipline us. This didn't excuse his behavior but at least it explained it so that I could know it wasn't our fault.

Not long after our conversation I realized in spite of all I had gone through I had become my father. I was beating my kids, drinking all the time, didn't have a good job, was living on welfare, and in government housing. Like him I was just trying to make it. I too understood the pressure and the stress. But I did what I never saw my parents do I got on my knees and prayed to God to help me. In doing so I stopped beating my kids and learned how to properly punish them.

The lesson here is that we have to take back our lives. We can't allow our past hurts to keep us from what God has for us. I ask myself sometimes where I would be now if I had not forgiven my dad. We have a nice relationship now and even though a lot has happened in the past I will not allow the devil that kind of power over my life. I won't keep reliving my past. When you can look at any hurtful experience that comes your way and say God has a purpose in this, you are on your way to developing a forgiving spirit. God has a purpose for all things. That purpose may be to do work in the life of the person who has wronged you. It may be to make you stronger. It may be to perfect an area in your life. But mostly it is to teach you to have a forgiving spirit!

I want to say this because it helped me. In Matthew 18:21 it says, "Lord how often shall my brother sin against me, and I forgive Him? Up to seven times.

Jesus saith unto him, "I say not unto thee, until seven times; but until seventy times seven."

I say let go of the guilt we hold towards ourselves because from God's perspective there is no accountability placed upon the other person for what happened. True guilt is associated with willful sin, not sin that is against one's will. Love yourself enough to free yourself

To Whom Honor is Due

Honor thy father and thy mother: that thy days may be long upon the land which the Lord thy God giveth thee....Exodus 20: 12 KJV

This request from God weighs heavy on the hearts of many children who have been abused by their parents. The idea of rewarding abusers with honor seems completely unreasonable and inconsistent to just about everything else written in the Bible, where evildoers are never honored, but instead are punished for their wrongdoing.

Although we are told to submit to governing authorities, the Scriptures contain numerous references to confronting, disobeying, fighting against, and even overthrowing ungodly, unjust, or wicked authorities. One of the most interesting accounts of a child defying his father starts in 1 Samuel, where we begin to read the story of David, who slew Goliath and became a faithful servant of King Saul. Saul's son Jonathan loved David as if he was his own brother (1 Samuel 18: 1-4). Saul became jealous of David's heroic exploits and popularity with the people, and wanted to kill him (1 Samuel 18: 1:15, 25, 29; 1 Samuel 19, etc.) Even though David had always been loyal to Saul, and even spared Saul's life when he had the opportunity to kill him that didn't stop Saul's wrath. (1 Samuel 24).

Jonathan, Saul's son protected David, helped him to hide, and tried to act as a go-between between him and Saul to make peace. Saul's anger rose against his own son and he said to him, "You son of a perverse and rebellious woman! Don't I know that you have sided with the son of Jesse to your own shame and to the shame of the mother who bore you? As long as the son of Jesse lives on this earth, neither you nor your kingdom will be established. Now send and bring him to me, for he must die!" "Why should he be put to death? What has he done?" Jonathan asked his father. But Saul hurled his spear at him to kill him. Then Jonathan knew that his father intended to kill David. Jonathan got up from the table in fierce anger; on that second day of the month, he did not eat, because he was grieved at his father's shameful treatment of David."....1 Samuel 20: 30-34 NIV.

Jonathan was ashamed of his father's behavior. When Jonathan believed that his father was being unjust, he confronted him. When Jonathan realized that his father intended to kill David, he defied him. The next day he warned David and protected him by allowing him to escape to Nob. At great personal cost to himself (the loss of his own kingdom), Jonathan stepped in and stopped his father from doing wrong and hurting an innocent person. He did not show honor to his father- he showed "fierce anger". Jonathan did not obey his father. Instead, he did the right thing and stopped his father's plans.

Jonathan did not think in terms of "He's my father, right or wrong, and I have to honor him and do whatever he wants me to do". In fact, when given the choice between doing what was right and obeying his abusive father, he betrayed his father. Jonathan publicly disagreed with his father, expressed fierce anger to his father, and then went behind his father's back to do the right thing and save David. And thanks to him, David went on to become king, and a cornerstone of the history of our faith. Jonathan is a biblical hero, not for "honoring" his father, but for standing up to his father and taking action AGAINST him, because what his father was doing was WRONG, and Jonathan would not allow it.

Jonathan's story illustrates that "honoring" as referred to in Scriptures does not mean letting our abusive parents get away with anything they want, no matter how harmful, without ever stopping them, or at least making them live with the consequences of their own actions.

One of the best ways to honor someone is to help them be the very best person that they can be. Some people need a little push along the path to righteousness and godliness. Allowing God's law of Sowing and Reaping to bring evil people to repentance is more beneficial to them than interfering with the Natural Consequences of their behavior by giving them a free ride. The Bible tells us to rebuke evil and try to turn sinners from their wicked ways in the hopes of saving them (Ezekiel 33:7-9). This is the biggest favor and honor we could do for them.

Many of us still love our abusers, but because it is not safe to be with them, we have learned to love them from a distance. The same is true of honoring. If your parents refuse to respect your boundaries and choose to continue mistreating you, then you can limit or end, if necessary, your time with them, "honor" them from a safe distance, and still be obedient to God's Word. You can speak the truth about your parents at all times and not be dishonoring them. Only people who want carte blanche to get away with anything would accuse you of not honoring them simply because you spoke the truth and set healthy boundaries in your relationship.

A lot of damage has been done in the name of obedience, by insisting that abused children ignore their pain and heap false praise on their parents. Abuse is sinful (Deuteronomy 6:6-7, Ephesians 6:4). However, it is possible to acknowledge abuse and discover ways in which you're capable of showing honor to your parents. This will depend on the work you do to heal, the ability of the parent to admit the abuse, as well as the level of abuse. Christian counseling can help in addition to developing deep spiritual friendships within which you can tell your story and rebuild trust.

SURVIVING DARKNESS

Ramona Pearcey Burnett

In 2009, I underwent a routine gynecological procedure that was meant to improve my chances of conceiving a child. Weeks after this surgery I learned that I had cancer. To add insult to injury the final report indicated I had two forms; ovarian and uterine. The doctors were not looking for cancer, so they did not determine the stage of the disease in the preliminary diagnosis. Not knowing the cancer stage meant I had to take the most aggressive treatment route. My only option was to have a full hysterectomy and begin chemotherapy, which, of course, would leave me unable to conceive. All I ever wanted to be was a mother, so letting this dream die would be the hardest thing I had ever done.

After the diagnosis, my husband, Anthony and I could barely talk to each other without crying. The air in our home was humid from all of our tears. I hated to see my reflection in his eyes, because all I saw was my failure. I had failed to give him a child. Our wedding day had only been celebrated a little over a year so this was a big test for our young marriage. There is no sadness like that between a husband and a wife. Through our tears we held on to each other and reminded each other that we vowed to love even in sickness and health.

During one of my pre -op appointments, the doctors were talking to us about survival rates—survival rates! I was only 43 years old! Forty-three was too young to die. I panicked, my heart seized, and I had to make myself breathe. At that moment, I heard God say to me, "You do not have time to be sad, angry, pitiful or scared. You only have time to fight. You cannot sit in this desert of grief – and live. You will have to fight." Until then my sadness had been about losing the chance to be a mother. Throughout this ordeal I assumed I would live, but now it registered with me that I would have to fight to do so. Fighting cancer would be impossible when all I thought about was not being able to have a baby. I put all baby thoughts aside and concentrated on my health. After all there was still another surgery, recovery and chemo to deal with and for me that was enough.

Before undergoing the hysterectomy, I became a prayer warrior. I sat in my home and prayed aloud several times during the day. I prayed for God's help in even the simple things. I was thankful and upbeat in my prayers. My strength was renewed through my prayers and the prayers of my friends and family. My battle plan was to take exceptional care of myself. In addition to praying, I slept as much as possible. I ate well despite the fact that chemo makes everything taste like aluminum foil! My doctors had me on a lot of pills to manage my pain and keep my energy levels up. I followed their instructions to the letter – which is rare for me. I was a warrior and prepared to win.

Chemotherapy wiped me out physically. The pain from the treatments was in my bones, and it hurt like nothing I had ever felt. No pain pill would put a dent in the ache that I felt all over my body. I felt like my bones were being stretched. To get through the treatments and the pain I prayed constantly. I prayed while I leaned over the sink to brush my teeth, "Dear Lord I feel dizzy, please keep me upright. Thank you,

Lord." I prayed to be able to eat, "Father, I cannot take the taste of anything, please help me to get this meal down and keep it down." During those times that I could not find words to pray I just hummed. Finally, at the very end of my strength I prayed for the chemo to end and my doctors decided that five rounds were enough! All I could say was Hallelujah!

The physical war was won, and now it was back to the business of everyday living in a life that did not resemble anything that I had planned. I now had to wrestle with not being able to have a child. I felt empty. I thought of myself as a desert. I was dry and dusty. I doubted my husband's love for me in those days. I was inconsolable and hard to be around even for those who loved me most. I had battled cancer, but was about to lose the war with depression. I could not see a mother and child without feeling a knife in my heart. Cancer was gone, but bitterness was seeping into my heart. Where was my warrior spirit?

After my first cancer free checkup, Anthony and I decided to investigate the foster care system. We thought foster care would be a good option because it seemed like a quick way to bring a child into our home.

We soon learned that for us at least navigating the foster care system would not be easy. We submitted to countless visits and tests. Our contact told us to be ready on any given Friday to take in a child and be prepared to return the child to the agency within days. Our hearts were too tender for this revolving door. After months of inspections and preparations we knew that foster care was not what God had for us. We were anxious. We were trying to make our family in our own strength and we were not strong enough to do so.

If foster care would not work, we thought perhaps adoption would be better suited for us. I contacted an agency and got the ball rolling. This agency was filled with people who seemed to want to help us. Again, we filled out tons of paperwork and attended many meetings. Then we sent a big check only to find that more and more checks would be needed to adopt a child through this agency. One night Anthony and I sat close, and the tears just came for both of us. Maybe it was just supposed to be the two of us. We held each other and decided to let the dream go. We prayed and agreed that God would bring us whatever we were supposed to have and if that meant no children we would be happy with that as well.

With Anthony's blessing, I put out one last plea to our friends and family. I sent an email asking our friends to pray that we would be blessed with a child. I also asked a couple of our friends who were in ministry to think of us if they learned of a child in need of adoption. That was it.

A couple of years passed and at this point I was well into my forties and Anthony was 50. We were beyond the preferred age of most adoption agencies. We had started to think about how we would live out the rest of our lives. Finally, we were at peace. We were content. The longing had gone, and we were concentrating on Anthony's adult daughter and her eight year old daughter. Then one Saturday evening I got a text from a dear friend in Fort Worth asking me to please read my email. I thought it was just another recipe or outfit to critique. It wasn't. The email had a blurry picture of a little angel and stated that an adoption agency was looking for a good home for her. I don't think I was breathing while I read the email. I forwarded the email to Anthony, and he agreed that we should get more information.

Weeks later we met the birth family and the baby at a local restaurant. I don't think I have ever been more nervous but happy at the same time. As we sat and ate dinner, I kept trying to see this child as my child. She was withdrawn and sullen. Her mother was there with several of her other children. I could tell she was tired and in her words "out of love". By the time dinner was over my heart was beginning to feel the familiar ache and I was kicking myself for trying again. This child would not even look at us. Surely, the mother and the social worker would not see a match here. Just before walking out the door Anthony reached down and lifted the baby up in the air. Deep dimples that I hadn't seen before erupted in that little chocolate face and a giggle bubbled up from her tummy. That was it. From that moment on she lit up each time we visited with her. We met with the family a couple more times and on January 23, 2014, Lamona came to live with us. She has filled our hearts and our home with more love than I thought we could hold.

On May 9, 2014, we finalized the adoption of our daughter Lamona Jewel. It was as if she understood what was happening on that Friday in San Antonio. I am a mom not in spite of everything that came my way, but rather because it was God's plan from the beginning. I was born for this. I won for this. Lamona was born to be my daughter.

When we stopped trying and allowed God to bring the BEST to our lives, he delivered. We could have continued with the foster care agency but while it is for some it was not for us. We could have bankrupted ourselves with the first adoption opportunity, but that was not for us. God had the perfect timing and situation for us.

As it turns out cancer doesn't always win or kill dreams. In my case, I learned some life changing lessons from fighting cancer. My scars are visible on my body, but my healing is on the inside. My healing and my lessons are safely tucked away in my heart and mind ready for the next battle. There is one lesson that I am reminded of each morning by none other than Lamona Jewel. When she wakes up each morning she runs to me and says, "Look Mommy the dark blow away." And she is right. The dark always blows away and with that comes joy.

BARREN ON PURPOSE

For I know the plans I have for you," declares the LORD, "plans to prosper you and not to harm you, plans to give you hope and a future. Jeremiah 29:11 KJV

Scripture identifies several women for whom we do not now their motherhood. For these women the lack of motherhood and or infertility is not the central point of their lives. Most of these women were faithful to their God and are prime examples of remarkable service. Their commitment to God and their willingness to give their lives purpose and meaning by searching out and fulfilling God's plan for them is both empowering and inspiring.

Even though it appears children were not part of that plan women like Pharaoh's daughter, the woman who adopted Moses, most definitely played an integral role in God's divine plan. Though she was surely a worshipper of Egyptian idols, God chose her to protect the Hebrew child who would be the liberator of His enslaved people. When you see her reaction to finding a three-month-old slave-child in a basket on the Nile, we can only wonder if her deep mercy was a result of her deep pain of infertility.

Then there is Priscilla who along with her husband Aquila, became great friends with Paul and exceptional leaders in the new church. Though she is never labeled as barren, neither are her offspring ever mentioned. Five of seven times she is listed before Aquila, which may indicate she carried the greater responsibility in the church. Her life may have been childless, but it was not empty or purposeless. Instead, along with her husband she made eternal contributions to the first century Christian church.

Lastly there is Dorcas or Tabitha. This woman was known for her ministry of sharing with widows and fatherless children. We don't know her age, but we can wonder if she, too, was a childless widow, since neither husband nor children are mentioned. Her gift is her ability to sew clothing for the needy. When she dies suddenly, the disciples send for Peter, who had just arrived in nearby Lydda. He came to Joppa and restored Dorcas to life and ministry. (See Acts 9:36-

42.) This lets us know just how important she was to the body of Christ.

Being childless can be a difficult reality to accept. Some may even become consumed with it. So much so that their longing for a child can eventually swallow up the joy in their lives. Money and time are no object in their pursuit to adopt or become pregnant. They will do anything, make any sacrifice, to have a child. Disappointment and the prospect of unrealized expectations may cause them to be uncomfortable with those who are blessed with children. They may find fault with each other or become angry with themselves. They may doubt God's wisdom as it applies to their lives. These are real feelings.

Not having a child can indeed be a tough pill to swallow, but it is never hopeless. The extent of a Christian's earthly hopes is always, Be it as God wills. God has a plan for all of us, even the childless. In Ephesians 1:11-12, we read, "In him we were also chosen, having been predestined according to the plan of him who works out everything in conformity with the purpose of his will, in order that we, who were the first to hope in Christ, might be for the praise of his glory."

There is much comfort in those words. They remind us that God has chosen us to be his own in and through the work of Christ Jesus. They remind us that everything is in conformity with God's purpose and will, even childlessness. Not having children will somehow serve God's purpose and bring glory to the Savior's name. Coping requires that kind of comfort. How wonderful to know that our lives are not off track. Within God's plan everything fits together perfectly.

FROM STRUGGLE TO FREEDOM

Cee Cee H. Caldwell-Miller

Lights, Camera and Action, are the words I dreamed of hearing as I fulfilled my childhood dream of being on the television or movie screen. From the beginning of my life, all I really wanted to do was entertain people through performance art. No one could tell me anything different. However, life had an alternate plan for me. I wanted people to love, admire and respect me. I wanted to make people happy and wanted to help them in any way I could. But my life did not happen quite the way I had anticipated. You see, I came into this world kicking and screaming, ready to take the world by storm. I had ideas, hopes and dreams about what life would be like for me. I had felt trapped for so long. I wanted to get out and experience my amazing life but the time was not right for me to enter into the stratosphere that was full of motion and activity. I had to wait until my predestined God ordained time. I had to wait until this place we call earth was ready for my arrival. I suppose plans had to be set in order, schedules arranged, personality and character traits defined, gender chosen, talents & gifts imparted, and the right family interviewed before I could grace the world with my undeniable presence. August 29, 1968, 7:59 am was the time for me to make my grand entrance into a world I thought was full of wonderment, love, happiness and joy. However to my surprise, that is not what it was like for me at all.

I had no idea that for African-Americans this was a rough time. Why, because just a few months earlier one of the most influential people in the world, Dr. Martin Luther King Jr., had been assassinated. His assassination devastated the world. He was a mighty man of valor, a servant of God and from what I know of him an amazing man that stood for what was right.

Being born to a single mother during this time was not the ideal situation at all. But it was how it was supposed to be. Both my mother and I almost died at childbirth. So, I entered the world prematurely fighting for my life. I was abandoned from the start by my father, aka sperm donor. This abandonment set in motion a life full of the need to be wanted, to be more than enough and to be loved by a man. My mother was left to fend for herself. She was on her own to care for me like plenty of women during those times. Life was hard and that is putting it lightly but, we were a family of three kids and a mother learning how to make it with what little we had.

I had as much love as my mother could provide. After all at the time she was dealing with her own trials. To me being loved was more important than anything else in the world and I wanted that feeling at any cost.

When I came into this big world with all its beauty, color, life and light I was full of expectation, dreams and possibilities. I was surrounded by it. When I took my first step, said my first words, cried for the first time, it was there. When I began my journey of discovery, experimentation, exploration and playfulness, it was there. When I went to school for the first time and sat down on those hard uncomfortable desks, it was there. When I answered my first questions, received my first applause, danced in my first recital, acted in my first play, I was supported by it. As I grew into my teenage years full of rebellion, anger, courageousness, adventure, fearlessness, risk taking and being a total social butterfly I was reminded of it. When I fell in "love" for the very first time, had my first kiss and heard the words I "love you," I was celebrated by it. As I stepped into young adulthood idealistic, hopeful, a fighter, a survivor, a trendsetter, a visionary, a dreamer, a trailblazer, an actor, poet, dancer and lover of music, I was endeared by it. As I accomplished great things in my life like graduations, job promotions, contracts, certifications and so much more, I was cheered on by it. When I got married, raised a family, built a life and a home, I was admired by it. As disappointments, hurts, death, losses, suffering, and struggles seemed to grow and grow and come faster, and faster, I was championed by it. As I journey toward greater things, it is still here and I will now tell you what it is: relationships. True happiness to me comes from building true, honest, loving and healthy relationships so that when you experience life's ups, downs and turnarounds, you will not be doing it alone.

Having people in my life was great but it did not stop me from making some dangerous, stupid and life altering decisions. Throughout the years there was struggle upon struggle, fight upon fight and hurt upon hurt but I survived. My life consisted of love and hate, pleasure and pain, life and death, depression and oppression. Even though I began to achieve many things, the satisfaction and happiness I found was fleeting. Rebellion set in as a teenager and I went down a road filled with looking for love in all the wrong places; wanting to be needed and approved of. From alcohol use at an early age to numb the pain, to being abused by men just so I could be loved, needed and wanted, never wanting to experience abandonment again in my life, I fell for the lies. I wanted to fit in so badly. I have been abused by men, hated on by women, I have been scorned and hurt by the church. Imagine that the one place where unconditional love is to abound and the peace of God is to reside, I was wounded. I was simply a HOT MESS!

I was living in a world filled with hurting people who hurt people in an attempt to release the pain and the feelings of unworthiness. As a child I experienced the feelings of abandonment, poverty and isolation because I didn't know who I could rely on. Being born into a dysfunctional family, as most of us are, with addictions to alcohol and drugs, would send an adult spinning out of control. Imagine what it does to a fatherless teenage girl like myself. It left me feeling unloved, unwanted and undervalued. I held on to these feelings not knowing how to express them. These emotions I had been carrying grew up with me so as a teenager caring for a mother who was sick with LUPUS (Lupus is a chronic, autoimmune disease that can damage any part of the body skin, joints, and/or organs inside the body) I was confused and disillusioned. My mother did the best she could for my family. I will always be grateful for that. But because of her illness I was a teenager who had already learned to take care of a home because I had too. I cooked, cleaned and did whatever my mother needed me to do in order to lessen her load. Yet at the same time I was dealing with all of the issues that face teenage girls. I did not trust the adults in my out of bounds life. My distrust was so deeply embedded I sought advice, counsel and love from my friends who were just as uneducated I was. Needless to say this advice did very little to help me cope with the test, trials and tribulations that seemed insurmountable to my resilient, strong willed, hot headed, yet brilliant, fearless, bold and courageous self. The realm of full-blown adulthood with the pressures, pains, pleasures and pursuits that it brings were not much different. By this time though, I had been hurt, abused, mistreated, demeaned, lied on, talked about, jobless, homeless, loveless, empty, exhausted, broken, scorned and just in need of a release.

Life is full of ups and downs and we often have so many choices to make about how we desire to live it. I was no different. I did not want to do the wrong things or hurt anyone in the process; I just wanted to be happy.

I remember a time long, long ago, when my life was just simple, I was young and I lived my life without a care in the world doing whatever I wanted to do. If I wanted to dance, I danced like the world was my stage and I didn't have to do anything else but enjoy the jubilant, harmonious, beat of the music as it pulsated through my body. I felt on fire and so alive. Then one day I saw him, tall, dark and handsome. I fell head over heels in love (or at least I thought I was). We became inseparable, spending time together, getting to know one another and just having the time of our lives. As time progressed, I felt one way about him and I thought he felt the same about me. To my surprise, he wanted to have his cake and eat it too. I was confused as to what I wanted to do because, let us face it; I loved him, at least as much as I could have loved him. I knew that I had a decision to make but I just did not know how I was going to make it. When I love you, I love you and that's all there is to it. 100% of me is invested fully. When he disappeared for about a week my decision was made and all I had to do was make it known. My emotions were all over the place -mad, anger, bitter, disappointed, hurt, devastated - until finally I felt nothing but emptiness. As tears rolled down my face I gasped for air because I was having trouble taking this all in. Eventually I was completely worn out. Finally, I made the decision that I needed to love me more than anyone else in the world. No one should ever miss-handle the gift of my love, which is intoxicating and authentic. Losing love is a sad thing but losing me is far worse. Remember I wanted to be loved at all cost. That's why I let myself be treated any kind of way. I was trying to convince myself that I was in control. But the joke was on me because I was selling my soul to the devil for what I thought was love.

While playing the hand I had been dealt, the proudest moment of my life happened. I met someone who would change my life forever. I met a man named Jesus who loved the hell out of me. I gave my life over to him and have never been the same. I was blessed to meet someone who created me to serve unconditionally, show others love, compassion, kindness, peace, joy, understanding, gentleness, and friendship. And that person is God. He is a great listener, encourager, coach, counselor, teacher, inspirer, motivator and mentor. In a nutshell, He is the divine heart healer, a vessel of Faith, Hope and Love! I am now free to live my life the way I was masterfully and wonderfully made to live it; from a place of pure authenticity. Oh how awesome it feels to finally be complete. He changed me into a woman who could love unconditionally, dream real dreams, serve others and simply live her life authentically on purpose and by design. So let me introduce you to the real deal!

In life we go through many different types of emotions from happy to sad, love to hate, joy to pain, and fear to excitement. What amazes me is that even though we have these emotions, the people in our lives seem to think we should not express them. We spend so much of our lives trying to please people we do not even like and who may not even like us. That is genius isn't it? Who in their right minds would spend their precious commodity called time and waste it on the undeserving. I believe that we need to go where we are truly celebrated for the magnificence that we possess, for being fearfully and wonderfully made, for being significant and for standing in the greatness that lives within our hearts and souls. Not merely tolerated for our flaws, errors, mistakes or the bad choices we make in this life. Imagine if you will, living your life on someone else terms, according to someone else's beliefs, someone else's opinions and thoughts. That sounds like a miserable existence to me. Our parents were chosen for us and deposited in us from the time we were born their view of life and how we should do things. I do not think people should do anything but what they feel is best for them as ordained by God.

Every day we are surrounded by people who are broken, distressed, angry, hurt, bitter and just plain old tired of living their lives in mediocrity. What do you do when your world does not exist the way you planned it? You pictured your life complete with the people, places and things that would bring you joy, delight and pleasure. You dreamed of experiences that would propel you to a higher spiritual dimension where you would live healthy, happy, whole and free. Yet, what you have gotten is struggle, grief, and turmoil. A life that has caused the light within you to blow out. It is time for you to step up. The world is waiting for you to show up.

I often wonder to myself, what is a person to do when they feel like they are living beneath their privilege? What are they supposed to say to themselves, when everything that can go wrong in their life seems too? At times, I have felt so broken inside with no one to talk to or nowhere to turn. Hit from every side in every area of my life plummeted deeper and deeper into a state of serious depression. How can one propel themselves to believe in themselves and know that they have greatness inside of them that needs to be unleashed? When I look in the mirror at these times, it is not a genius I see but someone who is lost and begging for the real me to show up. Then out of nowhere, I come face to face with the truth of who I really am and not who or what people say I am. I am a blessed creation, designed to effect change in this world by showing up on purpose with tenacity and a zeal for life that no human can tamper with.

Imagine if you will a world filled with people who are living there lives authentically by design with the sole purpose of being a divine change agent for humanity. The discovery of their soul purpose has led them to feel the unconditional love of all whom they encounter on this earth. Most importantly, they feel loved by the Creator GOD which teaches them how to love themselves no matter what.

My life…

A life full of chaos

Abandonment from birth

Struggling to enter this planet called Earth

At deaths door

A miracle in the making

Was destined to be here to live life for the taking.

Growing up not being daddy's little girl

Surrounded by sickness in the sad, sad world

Depression that makes one feel like I am drowning

Not knowing which way to go or what to do

The truth really is who are you?

Trying to fit in where you do not belong

When everything in your life seems to go oh so wrong

What is one to do when what they dreamed of seems to be slipping out of their view?

Feelings of emptiness, loneliness, pain, deception, unworthiness, isolation and confusion

The things people have said are just an illusion.

I am spinning out of control feeling pressure from every side

If I only had a place where I could hide.

I take a deep breath and then appear to be in a place where I can escape my reality

I escape to a place free of all devices: Phones, Internet, Electricity, and Heat

It is nothing but the ocean and the sand beneath my toes

The breeze through my hair makes me feel alive

Now this is a place where I can thrive

I see God here

GOD is all I will ever NEED

I can Be Free NOW and BE WHO I WAS CALLED AND CHOSEN TO BE BY GOD!

As I sit and ponder over what I have been through in my life, the people I have met, the places I have been and the things I have done, I wonder. I wonder how my life would have been different if I had made different decisions, if I were born into a different family, if I lived in a different place, if I looked a different way, if I simply was a different me. Thinking about my life, its tests, trials, tribulations and testimonies in an idealistic but, non-critical manner, I wonder what would happen if I could just go back in history and begin again. I asked myself where would I want to start and honestly, I would want to be born again and not for the reasons you may think. I would want to be a baby again with the wisdom I have now. Why a baby you might be asking yourself? Babies are free spirited, fearless; they are full of wonderment, exploration and experimentation. They enjoy life and have no troubles at all. Babies love unconditionally without regard to who did what to them and they laugh as if their lives depended on it. When babies fall they get up, when they cry their tears are wiped away, when they are hungry they are fed, they are held in high esteem, they are complimented, cared for and blessed. Babies bring joy to everyone they meet through their gentle hugs, and sweet kisses. They melt the most bitter, angry and hurt heart with their brilliant smiles. Babies live their lives in the moment; loving, playing and being their authentic selves. They are honest, pure and true.

Well I have day dreamed enough. It is time for me to live like a baby right here and right now. I want to be the Beacon of Light, the Creator designed me to be so that my life will grace this earth school with the indelible impression that my legacy will leave humanity with; passion, purpose, love and light. My desire for you is that you too live your life full and die empty. I hope that you know how special and unique you are. Your past does not matter. All that matters is that you were created by God and chosen to serve. It is time for the real you to please stand up. The world is anxiously awaiting your arrival.

SEEK GOD FIRST

But seek ye first the kingdom of God, and his righteousness; and all these things shall be added unto you. Matthew 6:33 KJV

For most of us we spend our lives chasing after what the world would have us to believe is a good life. We look for fulfillment in people, places and things only to find that more often than not they will all disappoint us and leave us empty.

We chase after what we perceive to be our purpose only to find it elusive and unrewarding. In our attempts at self-gratification we may look to food, alcohol, or other substances to quiet the unrelenting voices of dissatisfaction. For some we even look to significant others to complete us when the reality is that the only one who can truly complete us is the Creator Himself.

Our ultimate happiness will never be found in things or people. Our ultimate gratification won't ever be found even on ourselves. It is only in God that we can live move and have our very "being."

Scripture is very clear that it is God who knows the plans He has for us and those plans, if we seek them out and follow them, will give us an expected end. An end that is full of hope.

While counterintuitive, seeking the kingdom of God is the only way that we will ever find true serenity, true peace, and true contentment.

ABUSED NO MORE

Clara Peters

I t's Saturday. Time to head to my home girl's house to have some fun with family and friends. I don't really know why I am always happy to go to one of our friend's house. In fact, I don't know why I'm happy for them to come to ours. The truth is, the evening always seems to end in a fight with the hubby. Nevertheless, just the idea of having time with grown folks is exciting to me since during the week it is all about the children and him. Evenings with friends was my only outlet. Nonetheless, it left a lot to be desired. I never knew what to expect when it was over because, my husband's attitude always seemed to be off by the end of the night.

We spent most weekends with people from my hometown, along with his cousins and their spouses. Friends had become family. Because of our shared life experiences and the length of time we spent together neighbors and coworkers had become family too.

My husband was a jealous man. Very jealous. Lethally so. The poison of jealousy oozed its way into the heart of our marriage and I had not yet learned how to extract it. His friends would complement me because of how I maintained my womanhood – I was always a lady. But somehow those compliments offended my husband to the core. Playfully and prayerfully, I would try to assure him and instill confidence in him by telling him that the words were only compliments and the compliments were an extension of him.

He didn't see things that way. From his perspective, if anyone were to compliment me it was a sign of disrespect to him. If I graciously accepted, that meant a lack of respect to him. That left me in a no-win situation. I lost no matter what I did.

My husband never complimented me. I never felt beautiful in his presence, Women are emotional beings and married women need love and attention from their husbands. To know our husbands both love us and find us attractive is like wearing a suit of shining armor. The icing on the cake is to hear it – to have our husband's utter terms of endearment. I never experienced what that felt like.

Friends and family time was always enjoyable and on this night in particular, I was hopeful that there wouldn't be any issues. But once we got into the car to go home my optimism was crushed. He was upset – his blood was boiling. I had become so exhausted from the abuse, his rants and tirades. Yet, I endured it all because I didn't want to break my family's heart by having them witness my own personal hell and turmoil. I believed they would suffer in the long run.

While our children were asleep in the back seat, he hit me. He had learned over the years exactly how to hit me without the children finding out. I had learned a thing or two over the years as well. I had learned how to block his blows to protect myself. Sometimes, I was successful but most times, I was not.

My husband was drunk. Because of this, I needed to stay awake and alert for our own safety for the protection of us and our children. Even in a drunken stupor, he refused to allow me to drive.

Recounting the events of the evening he became more and more enraged as he fixated on the men who had spoken to me. A close family friend, one who regarded me as a little sister, had engaged me in conversation. My husband assumed the worst and the outcome of this innocent exchange only added fuel to the fire.

I wore my mask well. I was the good wife – good looking, well dressed, and well spoken, well behaved and well mannered. My parents raised me right. "Always be a respectable woman," they said.

The problem is everyone had mistaken my ability to cloak my abuse under a veil of a good upbringing to mean that I being taken care of by a good man. Nothing was further from the truth. Inside I was dying. I had lost myself a long time ago.

As we proceeded down the highway my husband's mood shifted. I could feel it. His presence became dark and my spirit became anxious. He uttered some words and all I could make out was that he was going to make me pay. It was at that moment that I recognized that he believed I needed to pay for my actions earlier that night. I knew this man. I knew him very well. I knew that the way he processed the evening's events meant that I had done everything wrong. In his eyes being cordial and polite to others was a sign of flirtation. I was disobedient and I needed to pay.

He pulled over in a rage and literally kicked me out of our car. I tried to fight, but it was a fight I knew I could never win. Not just a battle on that night, but an overall war on my soul, my spirit and my flesh. It was dark. I was cold, tired, scared, and alone. I was the loneliest woman I had known. I wanted to die.

Two in the morning and I was running frantically on the highway trying to find a ride and a place of refuge. I worried for my children; my three precious gifts God had blessed me with. Honestly, they were the only reason I held on so long. I was out of my mind. He had been drinking. My children were in the car. He was mad. The devil was present. I needed a miracle. I had to become a woman that would hurt anything and anyone that got in the way of my getting to them. I was mad but I didn't have time to be mad with him. It was now about making sure my babies were okay. I didn't want them to wake up to a man with a hangover who did not know anything about caring for them on his own. I managed to get to the feeder road without any issues. Once I got there I had to really put things into action.

I had been awake an entire day before this altercation so I was tired. I prayed to God for strength. I needed God to hear my pleas. I cried and prayed and I prayed and I cried until I felt that unbeatable strength starting to build inside me. I had to show him that he was not going to win. No matter what he did, I was going to get back up and I was going to have the victory. I was going to let him know that you can use and abuse me but I will win.

Walking and running for 2 hours I eventually found my way home. It was more than I would ever think I would have to go through. I encountered men whom thought I was out to have a good time. I thank God that one of the men urged the others to leave me alone and let me go. God spared me. Looking back I think that man saw something in me. I believe he saw that I was scared and trembling but I think he also saw that I was a woman on the edge. I think he saw that at least on this night I would have fought hard if anyone tried something anything at that time.

It finally dawned on me after they left that it would have been very easy for them to overpower me. I cried because I recognized they could have kidnapped, raped or killed me. Even so I managed to maintain my composure. A dream. That's what all of this had to be. Surely I would wake up at any moment and it would all be over.

Thirsty from walking and running with no money and no purse, I had to continue my journey home. Despite being pursued by an unknown man in a car, I felt the power of God all around me. The man eventually went his way and I went mine. God's protection helped me to keep pressing my way.

Because of the many people on the streets I found myself ducking and dodging the entire way home. I even came upon a dog who seemed none to friendly. My heart leapt when he started barking but thank GOD he was tied up. I only had a couple more miles to go. I was determined to make it because I knew in my spirit that God had not brought me this far to only bring me this far.

I took a minute and got my breathing under control so I could make the rest of the hike home. I knew once I got there I was going to have to climb and jump a six-foot fence. I knew it was the only window that would be unlocked. I was so happy to see home but I was also afraid. I did not know what he was going to do to me once he saw me. There was one thing I knew for sure I had to keep the focus on my children and off of me.

Once I made it home, I had to climb the fence and open the window to make sure my babies were fine. The fence was a struggle but I did it. The strength came out of nowhere and a voice whispered, "You can do it." Inside the house, I ran to their room to make sure they were all fine. I so wanted to kiss and hug them but I didn't want to wake them. I didn't want them to see how battered and tired I was. I didn't want to look at myself that night because I felt really bad that I let him do me wrong yet again.

Quietly I went to my room. He was in there asleep. Just in case he rekindled the fire and I had to leave the house in a quick getaway, I made sure to grab some comfortable sleep clothes. I went into the bathroom and cried for a while. I knew in my heart that this was not how it was supposed to be when someone loves you. Love doesn't hurt this bad. I stood in the shower for the longest because I needed the hot water to ease some of the pain in my body from all the physical wear and tear I had placed on it trying to get home. As I stood there, I reflected over what happened and all I could do was thank GOD. I didn't know my own strength.

I found myself drifting to sleep on the couch. To my dismay I was soon awakened by him forcing me off the couch and into the bedroom. At this point my only thought was not to make him angrier. I didn't want to wake the kids. In the bedroom he slapped me really hard and told me that if I ever disrespected him again it would be worse. He then threw me on the bed and had his way with me. I tried to fight him off of me however he was too strong. So, I just laid there and let him "handle his business." I felt so dirty afterwards. I couldn't move. I laid there and cried myself to sleep. Once again I prayed that it was all just a nightmare.

It was difficult to know how much time had passed. I may have been an hour. It may have been more. I awakened to him on me again. He was apologizing as he thrust himself on me saying I made him do it. He professed that the idea of another man talking to me just made him mad and his temper took over. I told him that I would never accept his apology because he knew better. I let him know that I understood that all of this was not about jealousy but control. I recognized at that moment it was going to always be "his" way or there would be consequences. Because I wouldn't accept his apology he slapped me and told me that as long as I live he would do what he wanted to do to me because I was his no matter what. My leaving wouldn't matter. I was his and he would always be able to do what he wanted to me. What he had just done to me was against my will and I let him know it. But it didn't matter. Because I was his wife, in his mind, he could do what he wanted. After all a man can have sex with his wife anytime he wants to.

My continuous disagreement with is positon only made matters worse. He proceeded to make the remainder of my day miserable. Even while trying to take care of my children I couldn't get rid of the constant thoughts of wanting to kill myself. Five years of consistent assault and battery had begun to take its toll. At least once if not twice a week, even while I was pregnant; it had to stop and it was up to me to stop it.

I so wanted to call my mother, but I did not want to move back to Louisiana. So, I decided to stay in Houston and find a job. I would leave on my own terms because I needed him to know he was not going to break me. He was not going to keep me in this life of hell. I would get through it. I would leave and I would succeed at being the best mother and person I could be if it was the last thing I did.

Sunday, the day of rest finally came and I asked myself how and why he could be so cruel. What is it I could have done differently? I had to realize that this thing with him beating and treating me bad was bigger than me and I would never know why he was doing the things he did.

The week after this ordeal occurred he made my life unbearable. He said I was not supposed to have made it and since I did he was going to make me pay every day. For an entire week he abused me in different ways. If I wanted him to go easier on me, I had better have his dinner prepared for him by the time he got home whether he ate it or not. If it wasn't he was mad. His pattern was to come home late every night so my children did not see the abuse because he made sure they were asleep

I felt like I was being his slave and not his wife. He took my being submissive as a way of controlling me. HATE became a very real word to me because that is what I felt toward him. I hated everything about him. He was not what I thought he was. Then I recognized that I actually had never really thought about him at all. I had just got caught up in the myth of marriage.

The abuse had finally become intolerable so I didn't care who knew; even if it was the children. I had had enough and I wasn't going to endure anymore. "Go ahead take your best shot," I said.

He replied, "I dare you."

I said, "Try me." He did.

I screamed and he slapped me hard. The kids still didn't see anything but they heard.

I never imagined being in a marriage where there was so much hell. I will never understand why some men think that because you are the head that you have to be so controlling. Why would you think that you could do whatever you want to but the wife has to submit to the unrelenting unreasonable demands? Knowing this inevitable reality existed in my marriage made me start an action plan. I was tired of enduring. My body was worn out. To help me cope, I turned to food. It became my outlet. It didn't help. Before I knew it I had packed on the pounds.

A week later the time had come for yet another gathering with friends. Obviously I didn't want to go because I didn't want a repeat of the previous week's abuse. As usual he beat me forcing me to get ready to go. I had a good time but it didn't disprove the fact that I was unhappy and abused. Even my unwillingness to participate incretin activities during our visit drew his wrath. In his mind I thought I was better than everyone else. I didn't believe I was better, I just knew I had a choice. So, I chose not to participate. I made up in my mind that no one would force me; not even him.

Needless to say he made a big deal of it. As soon as he could get me in the car he went there with me because to him I was trying to be standoffish. But at this point it didn't matter to me what he thought I just did not want to smoke a joint. I didn't want to smell it. I removed myself from the environment and I paid the price when I got home.

Continually allowing him to have his way with me kept me in a constant state of distress and confusion. I wondered if it was me or him that had brought us to this place in our relationship. Because he had managed to make me believe that somehow I was the one doing wrong. According to his actions I was like a disobedient child who had gone against his wishes. For that, I would have to pay. It was so bad that even if I wanted to go to the store to get a snack he would not let me. He would either ask me what I wanted or get for me. If he was feeling really vindictive he would simply say no. What he didn't know was that this food was my comfort food because of the way he treated me. Food became my drug and my addiction to help mask the pain I felt.

I overheard him telling his sister one time it's cheaper to keep her. When I think back on that now, I just laugh because if that was the case then you didn't try hard enough unless you thought that I was going to take being beaten for the rest of my life.

All I wanted in life was to be loved and happy in the way that God said we should be. That never happened. I guess I was living in a fairytale. I believed in love. I believed in happily ever after. I believed in the covenant of marriage. I would often ask myself is this the deck of cards I was supposed to have been dealt? Did someone else take my deck of cards? What happened? Why me Lord?

It eventually became very apparent that no matter how hard I tried he would never stop beating me. This fact was never more obvious than the one night I decided to go to happy hour with a friend of ours. When I got home an hour later than my norm he didn't hesitate. As soon as I walked the door, right in front of his friend, he slapped me so hard I saw stars. He reprimanded me for having him to wait on me to get home so he could go out with the guys. In my mind I was thinking, "He goes out with the guys every day. This was just an hour extra for me for the first time ever." His rationale on this evening was to show me that under no circumstance was I to think that because I was working I could do what he does. I couldn't go out for happy hour. You see He didn't like me working because he couldn't control my movements. He wanted to make sure I understood I still had to come home, cook, clean, be mother and wife. After his evening with the fellas he once again showed me what would happen if I tried that again. He had to be in control and that was the bottom line.

Confounded by what he had seem, his friend didn't say anything. He just walked out. A few days later he came by and apologized and told me he don't think he could continue being friends with him if this is what he does. I informed him that he had been abusing me for years and it wouldn't stop until he killed me or I left, whichever came first.

The man I married didn't believe I could make it on my own but I had to show him I was bigger than what he thought I could do. I knew whatever I set my mind to I would achieve. I had submitted to him all these years, however, it was time out for that. I gathered the courage and informed him that in order for me to continue being his wife things would have to change. He didn't believe it so I had to show him.

He noticed that my routine as a wife changed and that my routine at home changed but that didn't change him. After all the turmoil all the pain, all the tears I was beyond tired and nothing could bring me back to the point of liking him; let alone loving him. It was time to make a move: time to go. Somewhere in the mess God gave me the strength to finally move forward.

Life brings about a lot of ups and downs however we cannot just keep staying stuck in the same place doing the same thing and wondering why things are not changing. I realized that I had to be the change I wanted to see. I was ready to experience the life I had been purposed to live. And this wasn't going to be easy. I had never lived on my own. I went straight from my parents' home into married life. If I wanted to have a life free from abuse, I needed to figure out how I was going to take care of me and my children.

It took some years but I was able to get to that process of no return-no more abuse. I was taking my life back. I was determined to live for me. As long as I was with him that wouldn't be possible. He had lost my respect and he knew it. I grew bold and started going where I wanted to go and doing what I wanted to do. He knew the love was not there and that perhaps it never had been. By this time I was more reflective and knew that I never did really love him. I simply grown to love him because he was my children's father. I told him so. When that really hit him he knew for sure I was never going to be that same girl that let him do whatever he wanted to me. AS I gained my independence through working I also gained knowledge. Knowledge that a man that would hit his wife was a coward and didn't deserve to be called husband.

I prayed and asked God to give me the courage to make a change in my life for me and my children. He showed me the Serenity Prayer. I recited it daily. This is what helped me to release myself from the bondage I had been in for two decades. Loving myself became the main focus of my life. It helped me fight like before. I won. Being free to be me was my new mission because I had lost me in the marriage. No more abuse, no more bondage, no more using Clara for your gain. The more God showed me, I learned to accept not only my husband's responsibility but my own responsibility in allowing the abuse for so many years. Accepting this responsibility has allowed me not fall back into the same trap. Abused NO MORE!

FORGIVENESS

And when ye stand praying, forgive, if ye have ought against any: that your Father also which is in heaven may forgive you your trespasses. Mark 11:25 KJV

My experience is very similar to Clara's. I'll never forget the moment God told me to forgive my Ex. It was audible and it was clear but it was definitely not what I wanted to do.

I began to question God. I wanted to know why and how I was supposed to forgive someone who had hurt me so deeply; someone who was supposed to love me. How on earth was I going to do this? It went against every feeling that I had in my heart. Then God gently reminded me that He forgives me on a daily basis for sins that are far more grievous to Him than anything that I would ever endure. He reminded me that He not only forgives me, but He paid the price for my sins with the ultimate act of love: He gave His life.

God is so miraculous because my entire life began to change when I began to be obedient to Him in this area. Business opportunities came my way. Better job propositions opened and I was able to purchase the home in which I live to this day. Having a forgiving spirit brought immeasurable blessings into my life.

You see, God was the only Father that my children needed. He was our ultimate source and all I needed to do was release my will to Him. As long as I was relying on my own limited understanding, my life was going nowhere fast. When I placed all my trust in Him, the doors began to open.

Forgiveness is the doorway to healing and reconciliation with God and with yourself. One of life's greatest challenges is to forgive someone especially when that someone is close to your heart. They may not deserve it, but it is the only way that you can be healed from the hurt.

You must be willing to forget past hurt, (Phil. 3:13) pray for the offender, (1 Sam. 12:23) and give God the hurt (1 Peter 2: 21-23) while you serve as a channel for God's grace.

SATISFIED WOMAN

Nicolette Hines

It was not until I laid eyes on a graceful woman's strut that I noticed the chipped polish on my toes, the posture in which I sat in a chair, slumped back, legs a bit awkwardly positioned and the faint look of being unsure as a woman. I know why I was unsure just like Mya Angelou knew why "the caged bird sang." There were times when I would drink until I was completely oblivious to grace and modesty. I'm very sure that someone in this world can understand stumbling barefooted across a club parking lot, throwing up long island tea and wishing that just one cute guy would still wink and beckon. I was in pain from a dysfunctional life and clueless about so many things but who cares as long as I could drink , dance to a seductive reggae tune and smoke a little weed to laugh at stuff that wouldn't naturally make a funny. I had a journey ahead of me to transform from being disastrous to uplifting. Destiny was on the way but I was still undressed, unprepared, and blaming others for my failure. I was trying to be a grown woman but my experiences as a little girl were so traumatic until they were interrupting my maturity.

I was still able to hear my mother scream while they hog tied her and put her in closets, glass from windows breaking, police sirens and their flash lights shining in my little eyes. I can still hear the gunshot, scared and in fear for my sister, my mother and I. I recall being at home alone scared as a little girl while momma struggled with a drug addiction. I remember staying with her in a motel and accidentally stumbling upon pornography; tainting my innocent eyes with perversion. I still remember hitchhiking and walking the streets with momma late at night scared and trying to keep up with her fast pace. I often hear the distant sound of the blues from one of those old school juke joints that we would put quarters in and it would play café music from B.B king to Johnny Taylor. I was just a little girl who loved to go to the café because all my mother's friends would buy my sister and I candy, chips and pickles. I was like an old woman singing the blues and had no clue that I would one day drink strong drink and dance to the same sad songs. Momma is a warrior by nature and the devil tricked her into fighting against the good parts of herself.

She lived on dangerous terms and made sudden decisions without thinking.

A lot of times she made those decisions with me on one hip and my sister on the other. I'm grateful to have missed the night that she got in the car with the wrong stranger and had to jump out of the car on the freeway to save her life. Momma's skin was pink and scarred up everywhere with 3rd degree burns. Thank God she survived! I still remember seeing her behind bars and missing her because even in our dysfunction a little girl always wants her momma. The baggage of my past was getting heavier every year as I got older. Sometimes while momma was drunk I would be called an occasional female dog. Fearful of her anger and hoping she would not go overboard when chastising us I would cower in a corner full of angst.

I had the most respect for my elders and though I did not grow up in church somehow I believe church was embedded in me. I remembered one scripture that an adult taught me and it said that I should honor my mother and father so my days can be long in the land, Exodus 20:12. There was a rowdiness about my mother but there was also a very lady-ish quality that she possessed as well. Outside of her addiction we, her little girls, had to be dressed in cute ruffled dresses with matching socks, we were not allowed to get dirty and she was always on us about cleanliness. She would come off a long drug binge to make sure I was in school and staying focused. She would be hung over but she would not miss a birthday, Christmas or an Easter if she was able. If she did not have the means she was a hustler who would make it happen sometimes the best way she saw fit.

She was our protector. I remember one time she felt that we were threatened by a neighbor who approached her with a knife when my sister and I had just gone to bed. The lady and my momma were auguring in the living room and my mother had a sawed off shotgun. All of a sudden we heard a loud BOOM! My mother blew the ladies entire side off! The lady's Cuban husband came running into our house because they lived right next door and shot my mom in the neck. My sister and I were hiding under the cover in the bedroom scared with nervous stomachs and chiseling teeth. My momma came in the room, grabbed the two of us in her arms, told us to close our eyes and took us out of the house to a neighbor's house. Shortly after that my Grandmother was there to rescue us from the drama.

The entire neighborhood knew our issues. There was always similar drama that often kept me nervous and nauseous. For example, when my mother wanted to die, she pulled a knife on a police swat team at my grandmother's house. They pulled their guns and my grandmother jumped between the guns and my mother and said, "Please don't kill my daughter!" My mother's boldness often frightened me because it was surely beyond this earth. Nevertheless, she is still my momma and although there is so much to tell I have to remember I'm telling my story and maybe I can help her tell hers later.

~

In order to be a satisfied woman healing from strongholds and standing up to a conflicting past is required. At times when my mother was not around to protect me; I became a victim of extreme abuse. A victimized attitude made me unstable and vulnerable. The roughness of the struggle weakened my femininity. My voice at times lost its softness. My tongue became sharp and filled with filthy language. My emotions were imbalanced and I found myself blowing up at simple things because of anger. My heart sometimes cold and bitter and my character underdeveloped, I needed change to dine with my strongholds but only I could introduce the two. At the end of the day I enjoyed just being a lady, I dreamed of being loved by a man but I woke up when the dream involved loving myself. Every woman dreams of being a man's healthy desire. I often cried as I settled for being the main character in his fantasies by becoming a teenage prostitute. There is a difference between being desired for all the wrong reasons and being praised for all the right qualities. Freedom from shame involves enlisting ourselves to fight on the frontline, become our own personal warrior, and fighting for the good parts of us.

It is possible to have lowered the standard and still come out sitting like a lady. The way by which we experience life will play a major role in how we think.

It reveals the details of who we are. Now that I am older I value all of my experiences and filter them a lot more thoroughly than before. I've learned to get rid of baggage because I don't want my past getting in the way of my future. I looked for instructions on how to be a woman, her voice diction, her morals, her presence in society, her priorities, her emotional state, her values, her entertainment, her attire, her dreams, her company, her self-love, and her character. I was indeed a product of my mother's womb. Nevertheless, I grew to understand that there were parts of her behavior I treasured within my soul and there were others which I tossed away in the wind. In spite of it all she was destined to be my momma.

~

There is an aura that radiates from the soul of a woman who knows exactly who she is. I was missing that inner energy and I longed to be satisfied with it. I've read books and exposed myself to the history of women and learned how women have persevered in the face of great calamity. Women have made it through storms of oppression, stood firm and fought iron trials with a soft fist. Women have stood face to face with the devil and through prayer obtained the victory. Women have showed up in a man's war with aprons and high heel shoes to fight for justice. Women have used seduction to build dreams. We have submitted to being concubines and side pieces, some of us have conquered our fears and kissed the lips of success and others determined like Ruth have gathered other people's left overs just to make ends meet. I had to discover that we are more than perfect hips, lips and finger tips. I have met women like "big mamma" the elderly neighbor who took me to church. I've lived with her as "Granny" who showed me how to make it as a single mother with several grandkids whose parents struggled with addictions. There are generational patterns that sort of serve as a DNA blueprint of our "supposed" identity. A person can inherit dysfunction even before the privilege to decide otherwise and become imprisoned before the act of guilt.

~

I was supposed to be doomed because of my bloodline inheritance, addictive behavior, poverty, mental illness, instability, domestic violence, and self-destructive behavior. As a woman who was challenged from the beginning, I loved to get tipsy, hold on to anger, accuse my mother of messing up my life and find methods of escape that were destroying me, robbing me of true fulfillment. I loved to rehearse defeat and indulge myself in ways that were momentarily gratifying, but not eternally satisfying. Like having sex with multiple men. That is a deficiency and a dangerous appetite. I can't afford to walk in denial.

Eventually, I learned we cannot change the past, but we can take control of the future. It starts by getting rid of the "poor me" attitudes, shutting down pity parties, regret, and stop finding clubs to escape from the pain. These things only make matters worse. I had to realize that this healing thing is personally crucial! This is serious business.

This is only a portion of my story, yours may be similar to mine or it could be somewhat different, but whatever your back story may be always remember that the back story will only empower our legacy if we are willing to see it that way. It's all about perception. The word of God tells us in Romans 8:28 that God will make everything, even the bad stuff, work out for our good if we love the Lord and we are called according to His purpose.

~

"Charm is deceptive, and beauty does not last; but a woman who fears the LORD will be greatly praised." Proverbs 31:30, NLT

One definition of charm is a woman's ability to seduce, attract, or delight someone with her physical features. Body parts are only the accessories of a woman. If body parts were the way in which one would determine whether a young girl was ripe for mature things, then many would say that I was ready for it all. Looks can be very deceptive. When I was younger, I placed the most value in the shape of my breast, the way my butt curved, and how well my waistline narrowed in Spandex. I was already well endowed, having the silhouette of a sexy woman. I remember walking through my neighborhood and hearing the hisses and whistles of young and older men who did not seem to care that I still liked candy flavored gloss and roller skates. In a crazy kind of way, I started to respond to and crave that type of attention. I even questioned my attractiveness when it ceased.

I wondered why this perverted cloud was following me! Did I ask for it? The dark spirit of sexual violation haunted me at an early age. I remember one time, while visiting a childhood friend, her older sister tried to make us kiss her breast in a closet. I remember another time when I sat on a family friend's lap and he wanted to feel under my dress. I was molested as a young kid by pedophiles, not once or twice, but three times, and one of them was a woman.

People who have not experienced sexual abuse will often make light of the issue. I once heard a preacher say, "So what, you were molested! Get over it!" I will be the first to say that it is important that we get over it, but we must understand that it takes years for some people to get over this type of devastation.

Being sexually molested is one of the most confusing and shameful experiences an innocent child can ever encounter, being exposed to feelings and emotions that a child's mind hasn't begun to be able to interpret. Imagine, if you will, a spirit of violation that leaves the residue of perversion rooted deep within an under-processed mind. It releases a dysfunctional sex drive for some and a tainted perception of sex for others.

A majority of the time, pain is repressed beneath fear, shame, or embarrassment and left alone to grow without understanding. When this type of pain is left unattended to, it festers within a private chamber of the heart and produces an altered ego or personality that is a reflection of the root issue. For example, a woman of the night, a freak, a nasty girl, a loose goose, or whatever some may call her, is more than likely a victim of hidden pain from sexual abuse manifesting itself in inappropriate sexual behaviors.

Once a person is touched by the wrong hands at the wrong time, it alters their entire make up. Many do not believe that pain can take on personalities and become "the second self" or the altered ego, but pain will also speak to its victims and give them ideas that will cause them to live out destructive lifestyles. We so often entertain conversations with our pain and we become what it deceives us to believe about ourselves. There are so many real life situations that cannot be ignored; therefore, we must confront our pain in order to be reconciled to our authentic self.

I was touched and tainted! That made me angry! Had I not been violated, maybe I would not have laid with strange men for money! Maybe I would have managed my virginity and my self-respect better! I feel like I was robbed of what could have been! To be tainted is to have a trace of contamination due to something harmful or offensive! It means to be dishonored, discredited, corrupted, and spoiled, having one's name and reputation tarnished and to have abnormalities! In simple terms, I was a victim of injustice.

Women all over the world can relate to this definition and struggle to understand why they feel unworthy and worthless, and wrestle with sex and pornography addictions, fear of having sex, hating sex, promiscuity, low self-worth, depression, self-abuse, drug addictions, cutting, anger, lesbianism, alcoholism, un-forgiveness, shame, fear of love, lust, the need to dress provocative and be very seductive, poor relationships, adultery (unfaithfulness), masturbation and simply feeling carelessly strange to themselves and God. All of these issues have been closely related to the residue of sexual abuse. I'm not saying that all women who struggle with any of these issues have been sexually abused; I'm saying that women who have been sexually abused have one or more of these issues.

It's over! I decided when to stop being a victim and allowing my pain to live through me. I choose not to allow my past sexual abuse to continue to be my excuse to be tainted. There is nowhere to hide from such issues. Women in strip clubs, houses of prostitution, crack houses, as well as rich women, poor women, and women of all nationalities and religions cry out for freedom from the pain of sexual abuse. The events of my life warped me in a way that caused me to have very little knowledge of the class of woman God created me to be. I wanted to wear pearls and a white dress. I wanted my innocence, I wanted those lessons I should have learned when my mother was on her drug binge. I wanted someone to believe in me and teach me how to be whole and how to just be a lady.

Being broken is a major stronghold that weakens self-esteem and makes some of us unfit for the strong woman that is capable of building businesses, raising children, loving the right man and knowing how to handle ourselves in any storm or opportunity.

I did not grow up in a religious family and I knew very little about the power of God to redeem man. I use to feel that as long as we can get to the next church service, we will not have to stay too long at our own houses. However, we cannot get the victory until we deal with what's at home, hidden in the private rooms of our heart.

Too often, religion covers our character and religious people sometimes promote masquerade parties. Deliverance is a work out. It means we have to go ahead and face it for real. After the shouting is over, we have to get some journaling going, admit to some stuff, cry a little bit, pray a whole lot and allow God to settle that thing once and for all. It's like a spiritual detox. We have to soak ourselves in God's presence until we begin to smell more like His lady. I want His scent so I can attract the right people. I don't want no funk hiding in me because flies will find funk even when the natural nose can't smell it. Not only do we as ladies need the right scent but we must be aware of what we carry in our purses.

Big purses tempt women to pack unnecessary stuff, and sometimes the clutter can cause us to pull out things others should not see at the most inopportune times. What we keep in our purses will tell on us just like Freudian slips (when you accidently say a word that may be inappropriate but was on your subconscious mind). A Freudian slip is also like when someone call their spouse their lovers name while in the mist of making love, oops! The issue I have with big purses is that when I'm trying to find something I need, stuff I don't need is always in the way. Ladies we need to clean out those purses. Unpack the pain, the hurt, and the issues attached. I'm free and not only is my big purse cute but I have valuable stuff in it that is all in the right place. No more junky Purses! I learned to forgive myself and embrace the fact that I too can have pearls and purpose.

When something threatening penetrates the oyster's world, the oyster's natural response is to turn that negative encounter into a pearl, making the oyster very resourceful. It is also believed that pearls improve the quality in which we value ourselves and they also set the standard of how others should value our substance. Pious women might say that pearls are the reflection of a pure heart and the symbol of holiness. Those who wear pearls well may be stereo typed as the honest girls who wear slips, white panty hose, sit with their backs erect, legs crossed and whisper a polite thank you. I personally believe that all girls have a set of pearls embedded within them.

Today, there is a generation of us who do not wear slips, pantyhose, and while crossing our legs, you may notice fishnets and red hills. We wear deep red lipstick, we show a lot of cleavage and we wear jeans that are low cut in the back that reveal our G-strings. There is a need to be taught how to be a lady, mentoring on how to heal and be modest. I am prepared for this generation of women. There is a nation of women in today's world who are not the typical pearly type. God is the master of divine makeovers! I'm a witness that we can be groomed by our storms. The days of our past will fashion us to embrace our purpose, power and our pearls. Most women who possess a strand of pearls are not the polite type but with love, prayer and professional development, who will know the difference.

I have not always been the pearly type but today after seeing God take my life from insufficient to Satisfied, I marvel at the greatness he has graced me with. I find great fulfillment in speaking at women's conferences and seeing women who are battling my former demons get delivered and healed. I'm proud to say that I've authored my first book, A Satisfied Woman, Embracing my Power, Purpose & my Pearls available on nicolettehines.com. I'm proud to say that I've authored my first book, Today I know how to love me before entrusting that task to someone who does not have a clue as to how I should be handled. I'm an educated woman, an artist, a wife, a mother, a minister, author, a playwright and a counselor. God has healed me of my past and this joy I have is contagious!

Today, I can hear the sound of laughter from a Satisfied Woman.

A heap of joy bursting on the inside and exquisite glory glowing on the outside,

She walks gracefully in a room, head high, back erect, with confidence and class.

Many challenges she's overcome and she rejoices because she's free at last,

Character, Virtue, Bold & Unique, at times she wondered, "Who Am I?"

Smiling through failure, dancing on defeat and dreaming with tears in her eyes.

She walks through the storm not ashamed of the rain, fighting through disappointment and surviving all the pain.

Can you hear her laughter? How well is your soul? It's nothing like a kept woman who God has made whole.

It's hard to be happy with others when we struggle in our own mind, Run over shoes while living the blues and waiting for vindication time,

I long to hear the songs of a Satisfied Woman,

A melody of victory and the sound of one who is winning,

Ladies let us press past the struggles we've endured and become an entourage of Satisfied women.

YOU DON'T KNOW
THE COST

And, behold, a woman in the city, which was a
sinner, when she knew that Jesus sat at meat in the
Pharisee's house, brought an alabaster box of
ointment, And stood at his feet behind him weeping,
and began to wash his feet with tears, and did wipe
them with the hairs of her head, and kissed his feet, and
anointed them with the ointment. Luke 7:37-38

What must it have been like to have Jesus enter
a room? And here was this woman with an alabaster
box. It was her most prized possession yet she was
willing to give it all away for Jesus.

We can learn so much from her; what she was
doing and why she was doing it. She recognized who
Jesus was to her, and that there that she wanted to
withhold from Him. Recognizing that she had a past
that needed to be forgiven this woman knew that Jesus
was the only one that could do it. This woman was
considered a heathen by the religious, but she didn't

care. She gave what she had; she offered herself to the Lord as an act of worship.

Jesus spoke into this woman's life like only He could when he said, "thy sins are forgiven, thy faith hath saved thee; go in peace." She was in bondage to her past. She needed a breakthrough. She needed to be healed. She may have come in broken but she left whole. She may have come in in chains but she left free, and no longer bound to the past that she was held captive to. The Lord forgave her because of her willingness to give herself completely to Him.

God wants to give you a blessing that will transform your life. There are gifts, talents, and powers lying hidden away in your soul which will never be discovered until they are quickened by the Holy Ghost. When this takes place the prayers; the preaching, the unction, the power, the liberty and the Heavenly anointing that will flow from your belly can do nothing but set the captives free! Your words, looks, and your manners will bless everyone that crosses your path. I trust the Holy Ghost will reveal these things to your hearts and give each one of you a Mary-like experience which will not be taken from you

Beloveds be encouraged to go deeper and higher, to become more intimate with Jesus. The Lord offers deliverance to each of us. He is waiting for us to call upon Him.

VICTIM TO VICTOR

Letisha Galloway

I started enduring tests and trials at an early age. Both of my legs were amputated above the knee when I was approximately ten months old as a result of a birth defect. Some people had doubts about the quality of life that I would have. For some it was questionable whether I would be able to lead any type of "normal" life. People wondered if I would be accepted by society. No one wanted me to experience ridicule for something that I had no control over. It was challenging growing up with physical limitations. I wanted to run like the other children but I couldn't. It was frustrating. As a teenager I wondered why God made me like this. I was always taught that God was perfect and never made mistakes. However I thought surely he couldn't have meant to leave me this way. For the most part I learned to accept the way that God created me at an early age but I still wondered at times if I was a whole person. In my mind one of the best ways to prove this would be by having a baby. My entire life I always wanted a child. However, when I became an adult my self-doubt had me wondering if that was even an option. Deep down I doubted my ability to have a healthy baby. It shouldn't be hard to understand that after I discovered I was pregnant I panicked. Yet, the thought of bringing a living soul into this world filled me with great joy.

In 2001 I delivered a healthy baby; a son I named Jordan. He was God's gift to me and I was grateful. It was one of the first times in my life when I felt "normal". Before my son arrived I had never experienced joy at that level in my life. Unfortunately that happiness was short lived. My joy turned to despair two months later. My entire world came crashing down around me. I wasn't sure I would ever recover.

"I'm sorry for your loss," said the doctor. I looked at him and my body froze. I could see the doctor's mouth move but I was sure I heard him incorrectly. He couldn't possibly be telling me that my only child had died. It was exactly two months prior that I had given birth to my son, so no he was mistaken.

My brain was unable to make the connection to what he was saying. I was convinced that he wasn't talking to me even thought he was looking directly at me. I wasn't able to express the way I was feeling in words so, I just screamed. The bright hospital lights made me feel as though I was in some Hollywood production about a woman who lost her only child. Surely this was a movie scene and not my real life. I knew at any moment I would hear "cut" and the scene would come to an end and I would take my son home. It didn't happen. My son Jordan died at the age of two months and it shook my faith in God.

After the doctor left the room I continued to scream. I wondered where God was and why he was allowing this to happen. My heart was shattered. My soul cried. The nurse asked me if I wanted to hold my baby. I told her no. However, I did finally decide to go in to the room where the small, frail body of my only son lay. Family and a friend accompanied me as I entered the room where I laid eyes on my son's lifeless body for the first time. I slowly approached the bed where he was and burst into tears. I couldn't believe it, my sweet little baby boy was gone. My son who was once full of life and vitality was no more. As I moved closer I was able to see the reality of the situation; he was never coming back. I touched his face and his body temperature was dropping. A part of me was still waiting for him to wake up and cry. I thought, maybe he wasn't dead, maybe he was in a coma and a mistake had been made. As I placed my hand on his chest my hopes were shattered. It was obvious that he wasn't breathing. After about ten minutes I couldn't take anymore and had to leave the room. I was inconsolable. No matter how many people tried to comfort me it was of no use. I wanted my son back and if they couldn't make that happen they could keep their comfort. Some offered prayer and I didn't want that either. I had tried prayer and my son was still dead so as far as I was concerned God hated me and prayer didn't work.

The first few days after my son's death I was in complete shock. I didn't talk much. I cried and screamed for a few weeks. I couldn't understand why this was happening to me. I didn't think that I was the most horrible person on earth, so why was this happening? I searched for reasons. Surely I must have done something to anger God and he was punishing me. I tried to figure out what I had done so badly to make him take my child. I became frustrated because I wasn't able to figure out why this was happening. The more frustrated and depressed I got, the angrier I got. I was turning into a bitter and angry person. Anger consumed me. I demanded an answer and I didn't get any. Finally I completely turned my back on God.

I didn't handle the grief that I was feeling in a healthy manner. I was living in a dark place. I decided that I would stay there. When someone would mention going to church I would pretend that I didn't hear them. When someone asked to pray for me I would say prayer doesn't work. My reasoning was that I prayed for God to give me back my baby and the prayer didn't work. I prayed to feel better and for the pain to go away but the pain was still there. I was raised in the church and sang in the choir but after the loss of my child I didn't care about going. I continued to slip further and further away into a very dark and secluded place and that was exactly where Satan wanted me. My faith was being tested and I was failing miserably.

I didn't have faith that God was with me. I didn't have faith that God would bring me out of the dark place of desperation and despair that I was in. I felt alone in my grief. After the funeral was over all of the people were gone and I was left to deal with the grief. The silence was deafening. I was looking for people to help comfort me when I should have been clinging to the great comforter JESUS!

Within the first year of my son's death my life was completely out of control. I covered my pain by partying most of the week. Most of the week I was inebriated and I didn't care. Being sober was too painful. Being inebriated was so much more fun than being sober. When I was drunk I didn't have to think about the pain of losing my son. I could pretend that he never existed. I was slipping away and I didn't understand how badly until March of 2002 when I had my first nervous breakdown. I battled with my thoughts. I knew that God had brought me through other bad situations in life but I refused to believe that he would bring me through this one too. I was lost. I was convinced that God had forgotten all about me. I wanted to forget that my son's death ever happened so

I kept drinking and completely self-destructed in November 2002.

One morning after a heavy night of partying I decided to end my life. I woke up with my son on my mind. The tears flowed so heavily from my eyes that it blocked my vision. My spirit was broken. I didn't see any way out other than ending it all permanently. I needed the pain to end immediately. I had convinced myself that God would not be bringing me out of my pain so it was better to end it. My faith died. I was about to permanently fail the faith test. After I swallowed 75 antidepressant pills I stopped breathing. My life was ending. I made a permanent decision because of a short term high frequency of pain. After God delivered me from death's door I had a decision to make I could either continue on my destructive path or step aside and let God back into my life. It took another year and a half of trying to put my life back together on my own before I realized that I couldn't do it and needed God's help. As much as I told myself that I needed God's help I wasn't ready. I wasn't receptive. I didn't trust that God had a plan for my life.

After I was released from the intensive care unit I was transferred to another hospital that had a mental health unit. It was my second trip to this unit in 9 months and I was not happy about it. I was angry. I wanted to know why my son was taken so easily but my attempt to die had failed, I didn't understand. I was sure that God was going to let me die but he didn't. I should have been grateful but I wasn't. I felt as though no parent should ever have to bury their child. I was the mother. I was supposed to die first not my child. It was unnatural and I was not able to deal with the pain.

When I entered the hospital I was immediately transported to the mental health unit on the third floor. As I was wheeled on the stretcher I was overcome with fear. I was uncertain if the doctor would let me back out into society because this was my second visit here in such a short period of time. I had heard horror stories about people who were involuntarily committed and found it difficult to be released. The bright lights and long hallways were intimidating. It was as if I was being taken to a new dimension never to return. When I finally reached the third floor the medical personnel had to get clearance for the unit to open the door. I will never forget the sound of the door closing; it closed with a loud boom. The sound alone frightened me. I hadn't noticed the sound the first time because I had voluntarily committed myself to the unit for a few days. This time it was different. I was different. I was more broken than the last time I was admitted into the unit. As I was transported to my room I wondered why God saved me and why he forgave me. I had turned my back on him and couldn't understand why he didn't give up on me. I was in between being grateful that he spared my life and angry that he saved my life. In my heart I didn't want to survive. I wanted to lay down and die. Little did I know that God was not about to let that happen no matter how hard I fought against him. After nearly two weeks I was released from the hospital.

One afternoon in 2004 the Holy Spirit was dealing with me. I was lounging around the house and watching television when HE spoke to my spirit and said MOVE!! I kept laying on the sofa, being disobedient. I said "move where? I'm not getting off of this sofa whatever". The same thing popped up in my spirit again HE said MOVE!! I immediately got up off of the sofa and said it's time to move. I was overcome with emotion. I began to cry, a flood of tears. I thanked God for not giving up on me. It was in that moment that I was moved to submit my life to God in a way I never had before. I decided to listen to the Holy Spirit and I moved away from my hometown. I wasn't sure why God wanted me to move but I listened. I packed all of my belongings and within 30 days I moved. God was testing me to see whether I would listen to him or continue to be disobedient and continue to ruin my life. It was a difficult decision to leave the only life I had ever known behind but the move was what God wanted for my life.

When I arrived in my new state I was very nervous. I was starting my life over again. I gave up everything, my apartment, my job, my academics, and my friends to move to a place and start completely over. The change hurt. The pressure that God was putting on me to change was great but it was necessary for me to be who he called me to be. I trusted God. I trusted God to move my life in a positive direction. I knew that if he spared my life there had to be a good reason.

A few months after my move things started to change in a positive direction. I enrolled in the local community college. I passed one of my tests which was to move. I didn't realize that my test wasn't over, moving away was only part of my test. My journey through grief was still rough at times but it was bearable because of my reconnection with God. Even though God was moving in my life I still experienced doubts. I wondered if life would ever be normal again. While I was getting better I still had struggles with my grief.

For a long time I wasn't able to go to my son's grave. I would drive an hour and get to the graveyard and just sit there and cry. One year on my son's birthday I made it to his grave and I collapsed on to the ground and wept. I'm not sure how many hours I spent there but I am certain it wasn't minutes. I got lost in time. The feelings of hopelessness visited me while I was at my son's grave the first few times. One time in particular I cried until my eyes were almost completely closed. I started thinking about the life that my son would never have here on earth and I became overwhelmed and had a panic attack. The panic attack worsened because I realized that if I passed out no one would find me for hour or days because I was the only person in the graveyard and it wasn't a peak season for visiting such as Christmas or Easter. It was getting more difficult to breathe and I didn't know what else to do so I started praying. I begged God to help me. I fell down on my knees and then fell over. There I was laying in the dirt wondering if I was about to die. I was unable to speak so I silently prayed that my panic attack would end soon. All of a sudden a weight lifted off of me. It was one of the most calming feelings that I have ever experienced. In that moment I decided to live.

I accepted help. It was difficult for me to accept help. I accepted that I wasn't able to deal with everything on my own. I began to see a therapist. She was non- judgmental. At first I was ashamed to go see her because it was something most of my family just didn't believe in. You took your problems to God and that was it. Well I decided that God enabled the therapist to exist so I would go see her for my own health. Sometimes it is difficult to go against the grain and do what is best for your own life but I had to do what was best for me. I began to deal with my emotions in a healthier way. I found that writing eased my pain. I was able to express what I was feeling without fear of judgement. Too many times I was told that I had grieved for my son long enough and that it was time to move on. I knew that I had to move on but I was never going to forget my child.

After the prayer time with God in one of my most desperate moments a fire was rekindled within my soul. I knew that there was no turning back. If I didn't choose to live I would surely die. God delivered me from too much for me not to honor him with living my life to the best of my ability. I was determined to live the best life that I could. I learned to appreciate each day. I was ready to take on the challenge of life.

I transferred to a four year university. It was the college that I was told that I would never get to. As a child I was labeled learning disabled in all subjects. My only real issue was math. I eventually tested out of all remedial classes except math but was still told that I wasn't college material. It was difficult to accept who God told me I was instead of who society labeled me to be. Once I learned to see myself the way that God saw me and do what he told me opportunities began to appear. Not only did I finish my undergraduate degree I finished it a semester early with a "B" average. God was with me along my journey. He wasn't finished with me yet.

After I graduated with my bachelor's degree I was excited. God had more for me and I could feel it. I started to get somewhat discouraged because I was told by some that I should stop my education and go get a real job. I understood what they were trying to communicate but I knew what God told me. I was aware that I needed more money. God put it in my heart that I was to go further in my education. I didn't have time to question God. I knew he could make a way. I had to be patient and wait for him to move things in my favor. I did all I could do. God would take me the rest of the way. There were moments when I wasn't one hundred percent sure but I simply reminded myself of all of the things that God did for me in the past. If he delivered me from death's door surely he could help and give me the strength to get another degree. It was challenging and at times stressful. My retail job wasn't the best but it paid my bills. It allowed me flexibility in my schedule. With God's help I was able to finish. I earned my Master's degree. I graduated with honors.

Through the tragic loss of my son I learned a few valuable lessons. No matter what God was always there. He saw my tears he knew my pain, and just wanted me to trust him. In my pain it seemed like I was all alone but God never left me. God is faithful.

My greatest testimony came out of tragedy. At the time I couldn't understand why God allowed me to go through the loss of my son. I continued to search for answers. I finally arrived at the conclusion that it wasn't meant for me to understand everything at that moment in my life. I was supposed to just trust the process and know that God was with me. While going through a difficult or tragic circumstance it is sometimes difficult to trust God. Many times it feels as though he was not listening but he always hears the cry of his people. At night in my most troubling times God was present. He didn't talk to me a lot because he wanted me to trust him. Instead of speaking life to myself I was speaking death. I had to learn how to speak things that were nonexistent as though they were already taking place. I learned how to speak positive words over my life. I spent enough time talking to myself negatively and it was time to speak positively. I had to tell myself that "I can be successful" and "I will be somebody". At first I didn't believe what I was telling myself but I kept repeating it and over time I started to believe it and live it.

I've learned that whatever situation or crisis that I'm in God will bring me out of it victorious. It will not be in my timing but it will be in his prefect timing. It is at times difficult and frustrating to wait but it is worth it. God arrived at the last second. He arrived when people thought my life was over. He performed miracles in my life and got the glory. If I could have brought myself out of my darkness God wouldn't have received the glory that is shining through my life because of him.

Praising God in advance is key to my sanity. When I felt sad and lonely I encouraged myself and spoke life to myself. I told myself that God would deal with the situation on his perfect timing. God will never abandon his children. I experienced my breakthrough when I least expected it. It happened suddenly. Early on in my grieving process I didn't think it was possible to survive but I did. It didn't seem like the breakthrough was going to happen but when I put my trust in God and listened I experienced breakthrough after breakthrough.

My pain was for a purpose. I couldn't understand that at the time of my son's death. I always heard people say your pain is for a purpose. I used to think they were crazy. I was thinking why do I have to experience pain to get to my purpose? I used to think that God gives you your assigned purpose you accomplish it and it's happily ever after. I wasn't prepared for the roadblocks on my path to healing and success.

I discovered that God had a divine plan for my life and all I had to do was trust him through the process. The process is often times not pleasant. It is not easy to trust God when darkness is surrounding you. Those are the times when it is most important to trust God. I learned that if I can trust God even in my darkest of moments I can trust him regarding any aspect of my life.

In the end my faith carried me through the most difficult time in my life. It is what I hold onto when no one else is around in those dark and lonely times. I pray each day for God to increase my faith, so that I may face any trial or test that comes in my direction. Through my faith I was able to achieve things that I never would have imagined possible after losing my son. With God's help I have turned my pain into a purpose. My journals are now books. God is moving mightily in my life. God was able to bring me through the devastating loss of my only child. He turned my mess into a person that has a message. My message is that if God can turn my life around he can do the same for anyone. God is not through with me yet. There will be many more tests in my life. As painful as some of them may be I am ready because I realize that if there is not test there is no testimony.

DAVID LOSES A SON

And it came to pass on the seventh day that the child died. And the servants of David feared to tell him that the child was dead: for they said, Behold, while the child was yet alive, we spake unto him, and he would not hearken unto our voice: how will he then vex himself, if we tell him that the child is dead? 2 Samuel 12:18

In the book of 2 Samuel, King David has a child with Bathsheba. The baby is seriously ill from birth. For seven days following the baby's birth, David fasted and prayed without ceasing. We are told that he would not eat, despite the repeated requests from his servants to do so. We are told that he "layed all night on the ground" in ceaseless prayer.2 Samuel 12:16.

But after seven days of this fasting and praying, his infant son died. David's servants were initially scared to tell David. They thought he would be so upset he might commit suicide. Instead, after hearing the news, David immediately began washing, anointing, going into worship, and taking a meal. The servants wondered why, after feasting and praying during his infant son's short lifetime, he would act like this once he heard the news of his son's death. In response, David tells them, "While the child was still alive, I fasted and wept, for I said, 'Who knows whether the Lord will be gracious to me, that the child may live? But now he is dead. Why should I fast? Can I bring him back again? I shall go to him, but he will not return to me." 2 Samuel 12: 22-23.

David trusted God. He trusted that His infant son would be with God, His creator, in heaven.

Later in David's life, David experienced the death of a second son under different circumstances. (2 Samuel 18). This son, Absalom, was killed after Absalom's unsuccessful attempt to unseat his own father from the throne of Israel. There, unlike the death of his infant son, David wept openly, not having the same assurance that his son Absalom would join David in the life to come. 2 Samuel 18: 33

We too can have the assurance that when our loved ones who have been saved by grace enter into the eternal sleep they will be with our Father in heaven. To be absent from the body is to be present with the

Lord. And while this does not remove the feelings of loss, it should give us comfort to and a reason to move forward.

A DESPERATE DETERMINATION

Shamarian Bradley

I have come to the realization that the things which happen to you as a child can play a major role in the things you encounter as an adult. I am sharing this testimony to help others who have found themselves entrapped in some of the horrible experiences that I did as a child. People say all the time that sticks and stones will break your bones but words will never harm you. That is a lie from the pits of hell! The words that people say to you and about you will harm you; if you allow them to. These experiences bruised me and caused me to end up in some horrible places in my life. But here is the good news of it all, I may have been bruised but I am not broken at all! And just as God allowed me to recover well, so can you.

I grew up in a single parent home. My father passed away when I was five months old. My mother was an extremely strong, spirit filled, God fearing woman who I will continue to admire for the rest of my life. She took what she had and she made it work to the best of her ability. There were times when we had to go without the things that we may have wanted but we never went without the things we needed. I was the middle child of three in our household, having an older brother and a younger sister. My father had 3 sons from a previous marriage before he met my mother. So you do know that growing up with four older brothers was good at times and then at other times they were thorns in my flesh. But no matter what we were taught to love each other unconditionally. Now, did this happen all of the time? No, but we did our very best to take care of each other.

It was in my early childhood that I began to experience the situations and circumstances that lead me down many roads that I may have been able to avoid had I not experienced them. You see, often times we don't understand that for every action there is a reaction. And I can surely testify that my reaction to my childhood caused me to have several rough spots in my adult life. I knew that my mother had raised me to be respectful. She taught me that I was to not only treat others with the utmost respect but I was to respect myself as well. However, somewhere along the way I allowed my pain to cause me to begin a life of what I like to call self-inflicted drama.

As I said earlier, I dealt with things as a child that literally almost destroyed me. Out loud it doesn't sound very good nevertheless it is the truth. The good news is that what the enemy meant for my bad, God is using it for my good and He is definitely getting all of the glory. I was teased as a child. I know that you are saying, a lot of people were teased as a child. But I want to tell my story because every situation is different and I know that I am not the only person who has had to or who is dealing with the same emotional scars from the behaviors of others.

Can you imagine waking up every morning and the first thing you thought about when you opened your eyes was how many times was someone going to make you cry today? Are my family members going to laugh when these bullies start to make fun of me? Will my clothes fit too tight? Can I fix my hair in a different way that will not cause them to make fun of me today?

Not the typical thoughts of a young child, but because I was overweight as a child, had short hair, and didn't think that I was pretty at all, this is how I lived my life. There were days when the pain was just too much to bare and I remember lying to my mother and telling her that I was sick because I didn't want to face anything at all on that particular day.

One of the memories that I can never get out of my mind, although I am thankful that it doesn't hurt anymore, was the fact that as I walked up the driveway to get to the bus the boys would roll the windows down and began to make sounds like cows in a field. They even gave me the nickname of "mare." Nothing I ever did right was good enough to make them leave me alone for a day. If my shirt wasn't too tight, it was my pants. If my pants fit ok, my shoes were too tight on my feet. If my clothes made it for the day I had to deal with them making jokes about how short my hair was. It was never ending. And these were people who lived in my neighborhood. I still had to make it to the school and deal with all of my classmates and other students in the school.

Many children were happy about the bell ringing for them to exchange classes. But every day I felt as if I was walking down the hall of shame. I can remember walking by a group of older girls, who you would think would be trying to set a better example, and they would call me everything but a child of God. I remember getting on the school bus heading to a basketball game one afternoon. There was a young lady on the bus who was one of my classmates. She just happened to have severe body odor on this day. Now on a normal day no one would think of sitting in the same seat with me. But on this day because she had an issue that she did not want others to find out about, she came and sat in the seat with me. As soon as her butt hit the seat she said "OMG, you stink", and the entire bus of kids began laughing. The worse part about it is that I looked to the coach for some assistance and she snickered. Can you imagine thinking that you could look to the adult for help and you were able to find none because she was part of the problem as well? The young lady went on to explain to everyone that I must have been on my menstrual cycle because the odor was so bad. Here is the sad part of it all, I wasn't even menstruating, I had female problems that caused me to start later in life. This is where I should have learned to stand up for myself but I didn't.

I dealt with these issues throughout my entire school age years. I can remember my high school days as if they were yesterday. When I made it to the tenth grade I began to realize that there were certain things that one could do that would make people appreciate them. And that is exactly what I began to use. The very thing that people teased me about would be the very thing that would help me to get my foot in the door of the "In crowd." You see the older I got the taller and the wider I got. So I was able to dress myself up and could give just enough attention to the older men to get them to share alcohol and cigarettes with me and my friends. Although at that time, I knew my mother would kill me if I did any of that, I was still able to provide what my "so called friends" needed. Even if it cost me the disgusting feeling of nasty old men feeling on my breast and kissing me with alcohol stained breath. The very thought of it right now turns my stomach.

It's a very sad situation when you get to the point where you accept the foulness of life to fit in. Even after these friends got what they needed, I would still become the very butt of all of their jokes. I got so good with it that there were times when I kicked the conversation off. I had somehow become numb to the teasing and the horrible behavior. So I got to the point where I decided if I couldn't beat them that I might as well join them. What a very sad life to live, being both the accused and the accuser. However, the need for acceptance was greater than dealing with the real issues at hand.

Living in this place for a while I realized that I had to step up my game. I had to reach a little deeper to be even better for others. Let me stop and just give thanks that I have been delivered from this place. It was a very miserable place to be in. I am so very thankful to God that He allowed me to move from this place. I came into contact with a young man my senior year in high school who finally convinced me that if I wanted to be cool, that I had to go deeper that just allowing him to touch me. I quickly learned that it was all or none. I can recall the first night that I allowed him to have his way with me. It was the most disturbing place I had ever been in. I had no life in me! It was as if I was having a serious out of body experience. But if this is what it took to make me a team player then this is what it had to be. Every other weekend for three months, I dealt with this foolishness, to put it lightly. And what do you know? The very thing that I thought was going to push me to the in-crowd quickly became another level of embarrassment and humiliation. Struggle was the price I had to pay for the act of trying to be accepted.

This pattern carried on for many years after high school. Although the situations were different the outcome was always the same. Every situation left me at a lower place than I was before. Every time it happened to me it seemed like I was reaching a deeper level of hurt and pain. And I must be completely honest with you, living this lifestyle was extremely hard. There were many nights that I literally cried myself to sleep just because I was thinking about all of the shameful situations in which I had allowed myself to be involved. I remember thinking one night how much it would hurt my mother if she really knew the truth. I didn't know it then, but I definitely understand it now that God was allowing this thought to help me to begin the process of healing. It was time for me to face reality and get myself together. It was time to stop living the lifestyle where I was constantly trying to prove to others that I should fit into what they called the popular crowd. It was time to stop sleeping with men, drinking alcohol, partying and doing all types of things that were not right to make "them" like me.

I have always been in the church but I must admit that the church was not always in me. There was always something tugging and pulling at me. Although I felt it, I never took the time to respond. At least not until I came home from the club one night and was so intoxicated that I could hardly stand up. I remember standing in the shower and thinking I know that God is not pleased with my life. I can remember saying to myself that I needed to pray on one hand but I could literally hear my mother's voice in the background saying "Girl, don't you play with God." So I finished my shower in tears and I went to bed because I didn't feel that God would hear my cry. The next day was just a blah day for me. I was literally sick all day trying to recover from that horrible Friday night. I hung around the house and once again almost fell victim to the dreaded phone call of someone wanting to be with me behind closed doors and not in the open. But this time it was different. I wasn't even feeling it so I told them no, not tonight. When Sunday morning came I went to church and I sat in the choir stand knowing that I had to lead this song. The first song the choir sang I don't even think I heard because I was so busy in my own little world crying out to God saying "Lord, I can't live like this anymore." I asked God to show me a sign that I could be different. I wanted Him to let me know that everything was going to be ok.

As I approached the microphone it was as if I was walking on cotton. I began to sing the song "Even Me," by Yolanda Adams. "Lord I hear, of showers of blessing. Thou are scattering full and free. Showers the thirsty soul refreshing, whilst thou are blessing, oh Lord Come on and bless me. Pass me not oh gentle savior, sinful though my heart may be, I am longing for your favor, whilst thou art blessing Oh Lord Come on and bless me." By the time I made it to the next verse I was totally gone. The next thing that I remember was a bunch of older ladies in white dresses fanning me and giving me water. They told me, its ok baby, you are going to be ok. Gods got you now! And were they ever so correct.

It wasn't an instantaneous process but little by little things that use to grab my attention would just roll off of my back like a duck. The words and comments that others made about me seemed to be falling on bad ground. They were not able to produce any action out of me at all. I chose not to respond to ignorance any longer. People pleasing had a very bad taste in my mouth. And there was SOMEONE on the inside of me telling me that I needed to pick up my bed and walk. God began to allow me to walk in my recovery process.

For many years I have admired, taught about and read over and over again, the story of the woman in the Bible who had been infirmed for 18 years. It wasn't until recently that I finally understood why I loved this mighty work so much. You see, I feel that they left her name out of the parable because one day I was going to have to add the name Shamarian Bradley in her place. For several years I dealt with the humiliation of having to walk in front of people who were turning their noses up at me because I didn't fit their standards. I had to continue to live my life even though I had bent emotions and a twisted way of living and thinking. But there is one thing that this woman had that after many years of living the life that they defined for her to live, let me just stop and tell you that if you allow someone to define you they will definitely confine you, I finally got it. I finally understood what a desperate determination looked like. You see this woman didn't let the fact that she was infirmed stop her from getting to her final destination of healing and deliverance.

I wanted to share this testimony for all of the young ladies who feel that they have to sleep with a man just to get them to like you. I want my brothers to understand that you don't have to join a gang, or rob and steal to be accepted. I want people to know that humiliation, defeat and depression do not have to remain a part of their lives. I spent too many years of my life and committed way too many sins to keep this testimony to myself. Some of you might think that you have done too much wrong or that you have made too many mistakes in order to recover. But I am here to let you know that God will allow you to recover well. He is an awesome God and just as He did it for me He is able to do the same thing for you. So you ask "how is it that you were able to recover well?" I am glad you asked.

The first thing that I had to do was to admit that I had a serious problem. As if I was at a meeting for people with addictions, I had to stand up in the Spirit and say "Lord, my name is Shamarian Bradley and I have a problem." I had to come face to face with my problems, my faults, my fears and I had to literally face my pain. Was this an easy task? No, because no one likes to turn the mirror on themselves and see what they really look like. There were a lot of situations that I had to confront and overcome.

I had to address all of the years in which I had allowed society to define my total existence; it was all a lie. I lived a miserable life that was totally based on what others thought. These thoughts had me totally imprisoned and they affected the way I dressed, the words I spoke and the way I looked at life. All of my decisions were dictated by the standards of others. But it was at this time that God allowed me to turn the mirror on myself. I learned more of His word and I was able to see the truth. The Bible clearly tells us that when we know the truth, we are able to become free. God allowed me to see that most of those children were just being children. He also allowed me to get into His word to find out who He has created and called me to be. I learned that His definition of who I am and whose I am is the only one that matters. It was at this point that my life totally changed for the better.

God was continuously exposing the truth to me and it was helping me to truly recover well. I was starring low self-esteem right in the face and I now understood that most of it developed because I allowed it to. I played right into their hands and fell victim to their lies. We hear the quote all the time, if you give them an inch they will take a mile. When they were able to see my reaction to these situations, they just kept digging deeper and deeper. I was allowing them to push me lower and lower into a world of sin and shame. However, I am thankful that Jesus found me right on time. And through being open and honest with God about where I was and getting to the place where I could admit my problems I was able to begin a recovery process that has been a tremendous blessing to my life.

The second thing I had to do to recover well was to understand the importance of a strong prayer life. It is not easy to think back on all of the things that you may have allowed life to deal you. If you really begin to think about all of the soul ties that you created, all of the lies you told, the many nights that you cried and the pain that you may have caused yourself as well as others, it is enough to make you want to just hang your head in shame and never look up again. This is the place that I found myself at many times. It was at this point that I needed to be able to release all of this anguish, hurt and resentment. God has given us this wonderful avenue called prayer. When we allow ourselves to walk down the path it leads us to s brand new world. Even as I was still dealing with trusting others, I had to find the very One in whom I could place my total and complete trust. Through prayer I was not only able to talk to an all wise God but I was also able to listen to all of the wonderful things He had to say to me. Through prayer, meditation on God's word and fasting, I was able to learn the power of forgiveness.

To be a Christian, because if you hadn't realized it by now I had been converted, means that you must be able to excuse the inexcusable. I never thought in a million years that I would have been able to forgive those who taunted me daily. How could I ever forgive even my family members who took the time to mock me because someone else did? How could I forgive a teacher that should have stood up for me but instead decided to join the crowd? And even more than that how could I forgive myself for all of the ungodly things I had done in my life. It was in this process that I learned that hurting people truly hurt other people. And in my case I was hurting myself. I quickly understood that un-forgiveness would never allow me to make it through the recovery process. In forgiveness I found out just how much God truly loved me. I am totally convinced that it was His love that allowed me to experience true forgiveness in every area of my life.

During my recovery process God has shown me so many things; my insecurities, my weaknesses, and my areas where I need improvement. Some may say well all of those are negative but I beg to differ. Because just as He showed me the places where I was insecure, He took the time to also show me the flip side; I have security in Him. He has reassured me over and over again that in the areas where I seem to be weakest, I do not have to worry or become concerned because it is in those areas when His strength is made perfect. Often times we want to use people as our security blankets and this is exactly what I had learned to do. Because I didn't feel secure with myself I was always looking to add someone or something to add to me. But in this recovery process I came to the realization that I was exactly who God created me to be. Wonderful, beautiful and loving me!

The final step of my recovery process was to learn that I had the power in perseverance. Listen, there were several times when I just wanted to lay it down for real. There were several days when I felt like I should just go ahead and find a way to check out of here. I even thought that no one would realize that I was gone. But because I had learned the power of prayer and how much God loved me I was finally at the point in my life where I could easily say that "Quitting was not an option." I learned that perseverance combined with a few other characteristics, would be the very thing to ensure me a totally recovered life.

Webster defines perseverance as being steadfastness in doing something that despite difficulty or delay in achieving success. I had to persevere not just for myself but for each and every one of you who may be reading this story right now. You must understand that with Christ you have the power to recover well. You don't have to fall victim to the enemy and live downgraded lives filled with the negativity of others. I made up in my mind that I had a desperate determination to recover well and by His grace I am well!

STANDING TALL

And when Jesus saw her, he called her to him, and said unto her, Woman, thou art loosed from thine infirmity. And he laid his hands on her: and immediately she was made straight, and glorified God. Luke 13:12-13

Jesus was teaching in a synagogue on the Sabbath. Among his audience was a crippled woman; her body was permanently bent over so that she could not stand up straight. The woman's twisted body, permanently bent downwards so that she saw only the dirt. Imagine a life in which you only see the dirt! You can never look up to see the sun shine. This symbolizes people who lack hope, or see only the negative things in life.

But then something miraculous happens. Jesus called her to the center of the synagogue and told her she was free to stand tall. The woman, in her desperate determination to no longer be bent over, makes it to Jesus. Immediately her situation changes. Immediately she begins to see things in a differently. Immediately she is able to come face to face with those who had so often passed her by. This is good news! With Jesus' help we can lift our vision upwards, towards God, and be optimistic and hopeful.

There was a debate about whether healing was allowed on the Sabbath. Then as now, there are those who don't want to see you healed. There are those who don't want to see you made whole. But Jesus in His infinite wisdom argued that the Sabbath was a day set aside for praising God. What better way to praise Him than through deliverance.

This story inspires us to mentally and emotionally straighten ourselves to a standing position, where we see upwards to God for our inspiration.

WHAT'S UNDER YOUR RUG?

Esther Renee Wright

I want to first start this by saying, I truly thank God for the opportunity to brag on Him for the blessings He has placed in my life. I love God more than I would ever be able to express and you will see why the more you read. HE IS AMAZING and I PRAISE HIM WITH ALL MY HEART.

I wrote a book entitled "What's Under Your Rug" and in the book there was a chapter named, Name the dirt and dust that has been swept – uncover, discover and discard. And I suspected then as I suspect now, someone would be wondering how do you do that? How do you name the dirt and dust that has been swept? What does it mean to uncover, discover and discard?

To uncover is simply a matter of raising up the rug. We must literally pick up the mats to those places in our hearts where we have swept the hurts and the pains of our lives. Why would anyone want to do that? Good question. . . FREEDOM!

Freedom from what? Freedom from being haunted and controlled by unfinished business. The Bible says something; well it says a whole lot of good things. But, as I was writing this, a scripture came to me, "And they overcame him by the blood of the Lamb and by the word of their testimony..."

This verse says a lot to me, but more than anything else it speaks to an important aspect of our lives that is paramount to the Kingdom of God-- our testimonies. If we do not uncover that which Satan has been using to keep us bound, then how, or better yet, what do we testify about that we have overcome? The Blood of the Lamb was for all that we experienced not just those things that scream so loud they can't be ignored.

So the question is do you want superficial freedom or deep cleansing freedom that can only come from the Blood of the Lamb? The kind of freedom that when you walk in the room, you hold your head up not because you want people to think you got it going on.

But, because from the inside out, you do have it going on! Well that cannot happen without uncovering that which does not allow you to live a life of freedom from inside yourself. Maybe we need to look at what is the true meaning of the word freedom. Webster described the word freedom as the state of being free; exemption from the power and control of another; liberty; independence. Made captive, yet deserving freedom more.

This definition is power packed with so much. The first part of the definition, the state of being free, we have all desired to have this in not just some parts of our lives but in many areas. So when there is an opportunity to achieve that, why do we turn and run the other way? I believe part of the reason is due to not wanting to take on the responsibility of doing what would be needed and that is naming those things that have you bound.

The second part of the definition says exemption from the power and control of another." This part gives me a little problem in that it appears the door has been opened to blame others for not having freedom. Well, in some cases this could be an aspect of why freedom has not been achieved. But, on the other hand it could be that we have used the excuse that it is someone else's fault that we have been in bondage for far too long. When in fact it is due to being in denial, unwilling to even acknowledge that which haunts us, and most importantly knowing what is wrong but looking in the wrong direction for relief.

Finally, the last part of the definition, liberty; independence. Each time I read the word liberty I automatically reflect on what the Bible says in 2 Corinthians 3:17 in the King James Version, "Now the Lord is that Spirit: and where the Spirit of the Lord is, there is liberty."

I can honestly say that I know what it feels like to walk into a room and right before I step in, it is as if I have to prepare myself to do it. Afraid of what someone thinks of my appearance, can they see the weight I have gained, is my hair right, do I belong here? I would have a conversation with myself so that by the time I hit the door I have examined every negative thing I felt about myself from childhood to adulthood. Those very things that have kept me home on many occasions, missing out on life because of old messages

I have lived by. Don't get me wrong there is nothing wrong with wanting to look your best. What is a problem, is when that desire is consuming your decision to step into the room or not. I heard a statement at one point in my life that makes a whole lot of sense. The person said to me, "You need to stop judging your insides by someone else's outsides."

In the Bible there is a story that most people have heard at one time or another in their lives, the story about the Samaritan Woman, John 4:7-30. As I was reading it two things stood out to me. First, Jesus informs her, "If you only knew the gift God has for you and who you are speaking to you would ask me, and I would give you living water." What Jesus says to her excites me because it tells me that God has planned way in advance to give me gifts. If I could hold on to that thought sweeping anything under the rug would not be my option. Recently, someone made a statement that was very profound to me, the person said, "God's first gift to us, His VERY FIRST GIFT was when He made us in his image!!" WOW! Think about that . . . His very first gift was making us in his IMAGE! Then will someone please tell me why we feel so inadequate, useless, not enough, unmemorable, unworthy, shameful, guilty, resentful? Just to name a few. Because if we are made in God's image, we need to realize that He doesn't feel any of those things. We lack a very important aspect of our lives and that is confidence. We don't have the confidence to realize that no matter what is under that rug, God's got us, and He is going to walk EVERY step with us to work through it.

Jesus said, "If only you knew the gift God has for you." Due to where we are or where we have been physically or emotionally, how many of these gifts have we missed because our eyesight has been clouded by depression, sadness, detachment, isolation, fear, and ultimately a lack of faith? It is time to pull that rug up and let whatever comes out come out!

The second thing that leaped out at me was this unnamed woman's response when she leaves Jesus. "Come; see a man, who told me all things that ever I did: can this be the Christ?" WOW, do you see where I am going with this? She (we/us) had an encounter with the Lord and what? She (we/us) walked away asking, "can this be the Christ?" Are you kidding me???

Really? Seriously? Can this be the CHRIST? After reading this in one version, I thought maybe this version stated it this way, let me look at another version and guess what? In every version it does not show her running away with surety that it was the Messiah, she was still questioning if it was Him or not.

Isn't that much like we do? Because we don't feel whole and complete we are always asking a question to determine what it is that gives us the sense that something is missing. When if we could just remember the very first gift that God has given us, there would be no need for any questions. In most versions preached about this woman we are lead to believe that she ran away from Jesus proclaiming the good news, and in some aspects she did. But I still have to ask, did she? After all, she did run away asking a question and not stating a fact; and the Bible does not talk about this woman again for us to know what change, if any, took place in her life. I don't bring this up to dispel the way this scripture has been taught for years. I bring this up because that is what I did over and over in my life. I would attend something many times, join things many times, hoping that something would fill that hole I had in my gut. That hole that would cause the wind to blow right through me and chill me to the bone. That hole which constantly reminded me I did not measure up. That hole that even still today causes me to sometimes question whether someone remembers me or not.

I remember the exact day that I met First Lady Mia Wright, I remember where we were and the conversation we had. Every time I saw her after that day the first thing I would say to her is, "I don't know if you remember me or not, but my name is Renee Daniels…we met at Walgreens." The first few times she would lovingly say, "Yes, I remember you. "

Then finally one day I saw her, and greeted her as I had always done and her response was a question that blessed me way beyond what I knew that day. She said, "Renee' what is it about yourself that makes you feel that I would not remember you?" All I could think at that moment was, "WOW! How often did I do that?" I am worth remembering, but why did I not think so? What I realized was I had no confidence, no self-worth. As a matter of fact, I walked around most of the time with my head down. Looking at the ground, a friend of mine noticed that about me and gave me specific instructions.

That when I got out of my car, I should hold my head up and look people I passed straight in the eye, and say good morning, good afternoon, how are you? I need you to know that was one of the hardest things I had to do. I thank God for friends who loved me enough to lovingly help me to see the beauty God has placed in me.

We all have struggles in life that could make us feel incomplete, but the apostle Paul says we can be filled up to all the fullness of God. In Ephesians 3:14-21, the Apostle Paul made an awesome statement or better yet the Bible says it was a prayer for Spiritual Growth. This prayer if embraced can make the task of discovering those things that have convinced us that we need to hide them away easier to be pulled from under the rug. The verses read as follows:

14 When I think of all this, I fall to my knees and pray to the Father,[a] 15 the Creator of everything in heaven and on earth.[b] 16 I pray that from his glorious, unlimited resources he will empower you with inner strength through his Spirit. 17 Then Christ will

make his home in your hearts as you trust in him. Your roots will grow down into God's love and keep you strong. 18 And may you have the power to understand, as all God's people should, how wide, how long, how high, and how deep his love is.19 May you experience the love of Christ, though it is too great to understand fully. Then you will be made complete with all the fullness of life and power that comes from God.

20 Now all glory to God, who is able, through his mighty power at work within us, to accomplish infinitely more than we might ask or think. 21 Glory to him in the church and in Christ Jesus through all generations forever and ever! Amen.

What blesses me in this prayer is when it tells me, "Then you will be made complete with all the fullness of life and power that comes from God." Wow, is that a blessing or what? It tells us that we can become full and whole. So what does a whole person look like? Well, Pastor Charles Stanley of InTouch Ministries stated it as the following:

"They are generally satisfied with life. They feel loved and are able to love others in return. Difficulties and hardships don't devastate them, because they are able to go through them with the confidence in God. They are not complainers or someone who is quick to blame others. A positive attitude guards their mind since they know that the Lord will work everything out for the good. Listen, many times being a Christian doesn't automatically make us feel complete. Fullness comes only when we experience God's love for us."

Now I know you're probably wondering why is she talking about all of this. Because this lack of confidence kept me from allowing God to truly fulfill the blessing he had ordained for my life. Who could I possibly minister to with my head looking at the ground? Since I did not trust anything or like anything about me, how could I believe what God may have been saying to me? Like the Samaritan woman, I was walking around questioning, could it be God, really? I made no decisions without the approval of others. I can remember sermons I wrote that I would not preach until someone read them and confirmed that they were good enough to preach or teach. Everything I did was based on someone saying it was okay to do it. Who was I going to minister to like that?

I guess you are wondering what was it that made me feel the way I felt about myself. What made me feel not worthy to be in your presence, not worthy to believe that God was actually talking to me and giving me instructions? It was because I was living my life based on past experiences. Experiences that proved in my mind that God didn't want to really talk to someone like me, someone who had been where I had been. I mean come on... why would God give instructions to a recovering drug addict and alcoholic? Which He delivered me from and has blessed me with 27 years of sobriety to this day. Therefore, I knew he wanted me to help others to find out and discover that they did not have to live like I once lived. The only thing that had really changed was that I was not doing drugs anymore and I was not drinking any alcohol. Although my behavior was not like the behavior that went along with drinking and using any more, it was still weighing me down with tremendous guilt. It's like this…just because you stop eating the chocolate, the pounds you gained while eating it don't go away just because you stopped. I was still left to deal with all of the damage I had created in my disease of addiction. I still have nightmares and memories I wish God would wash from my brain.

Guess your now wondering how she expect me to figure out how the sweeping that has taken place in my life affected my life. Well, if you are thinking this is not going to be an easy task, you are right! If you are thinking this might hurt again, you are right! If you are thinking this might change some people in my life and more importantly change you, you are right! Getting an understanding of the damage that has been created and experienced through the sweeping of certain events under your rug, is something that can change everything about you. Your values may change; your perception of what you have believed most of your life will change. How you make decisions will change and your motives for the decisions you make will be different.

This understanding will do for you what you have not been able to do with all the other things you have tried. I am not sure if you are the person who has found yourself using outside things to soothe those ill internal feelings in your life. Outside things? What are outside things? Well, things like drugs, alcohol, food, sex, shopping, hording, isolation, sleeping, and depression just to name a few.

When the thought of how these outside things affect our lives we don't really see the manifestation until it is either brought to our attention or it brings too much pain to continue using it. Listen, it is not normal to do drugs, it is not an extracurricular activity. Using drugs of any kind is a tool people use to avoid the real them. If you think pills are not a part of that, please know that prescription drug use has risen all over the country. Pain clinics are popping up all over the city, and trust me people are not attempting to manage pain from injuries, but more so to manage inner pain. This inner pain is a product of not facing life as it comes, the issues we have decided we did not need to look at and were just swept under the rug. It is the reason we continue to use these tools, and I named them tools because it is a mechanism that works to keep us from feeling. Until one day this tool stops working!

I guess you are wondering how I know this; well, I know this because it happened to me. There was a time in my life that everything that I thought was no big deal, became more than a big deal. It became a HUGE DEAL! It became so huge that the day came that I wanted to die! But prior to that date of wanting to die, I was one who used many things to soothe what I did not understand. When I was in high school, I started using speed and my excuse was to manage my weight. Mind you I was not fat, but that is what I saw in the mirror. Desperately wanting to change who and what I saw of me wanting so badly to be someone else, look like someone else, I could not see what everyone else could see, and therefore the experiences I had endured to that point were slowly eating away at my insides. When the speed stopped working, I started drinking, well I was already drinking, but I took it to another level. Drinking made me feel one of two ways, pretty or I just didn't care, but it wasn't enough. I did not understand why I thought collecting Crown Royal bottles was cute, but I did. What's worse is I couldn't see that it certainly wasn't normal. I was then introduced to marijuana. Now I liked the way marijuana made me feel, but I couldn't get with how it made me eat. Because remember all of these outside things I am using is all about trying not to deal with the person in the mirror.

I think you should know why I hated myself so much. As hard as it was for me to write this, it's even harder because I have chosen to not share this with my mom. I want first to say to her, I do not want you to feel like you did not do your part as my mom because that is so far from the truth, you did everything you were able to do and then some. Thank you for taking such good care of me and loving me.

As I stated earlier, when I was about 8 or 9 I was molested by a girl who lived a few houses down from my grandmother with whom I spent most weekends. Since I did not have any knowledge about sex, I believed her when she told me that sex is "girls being with girls."

I knew somewhere inside of me what we were doing was wrong; meaning having what I thought was sex. So I certainly could not tell anyone, because I was wrong for participating in the behavior. This is where the shame began for me; this is where my hate for myself began. That is where lying about me began not just to people but to myself. The voice inside of me needed to be shut down. When I started finding things outside of me to help me do that, I overindulged to get what I needed. After that experience, other things began to take place in my life that was a direct result of that one thing I felt I could not tell. The one thing that was not my fault. I was violated and did not know it. This one thing gave me the feeling that I needed you to show me you liked me because I didn't like me and your admiration helped me feel good enough. At least until you decided to leave or our relationship changed. I look back over my life and sometimes think how did I not lose my mind?

As time went on I started running from me, in more ways than just using drugs and alcohol. I moved several times to other cities and states hoping these moves would allow my life to be better. But when I got there the only thing that changed was the place. Everything else was the same; I did not realize then that it would not change because the change that needed to take place had to happen inside of me. Until the day came that I realized this fact, I used drugs as if I were taking an aspirin. The problem was, when the aspirin stopped working the pain returned. Let me say this, I did not know what the pain was. I just knew something was not right. It could not be about the molestation because that was over and done with; no one knew what happened but me and her. So why was I in so much pain? I kept that secret up to the age of twenty-eight years old.

I was supposed to be in pain. For approximately twenty years I lived with this horrible secret and wondered why I hated me more than anyone ever could.

Along with all of the other experiences that came after that first experience, I believe there is another key reason that the pain increased in my heart and that key was the day I discovered my stepfather was not my biological father. I remember the moment my life changed, the period of time I was molested, and the day I was told by the person who I thought was my dad that he was not. That is a day I can see like it was yesterday. The minute it was confirmed that I had a father and my stepfather was not it, I was devastated.

I immediately felt different. I no longer felt like the "me" I was prior to being told. I no longer fit in my family. I didn't know who I was anymore. My mom, dad, and sister all had the same last name and I wanted that. I felt that if I could have that I would truly be a part of what I wanted so desperately…being a real member of this family. But, from that day I started a journey of attempting to fit in. Not just with those on the outside of my home but within my home. I can remember asking my mom could we change my name so that I could have the same name as they did. I remember practicing writing my name to see how it would look being a part of the family all the way! Well the day never came for my name to change. I never talked about my feelings around this major event in my life for over twenty years. Even writing this confirms even more for me how painful that was and sometimes still is. I'm sure there are some other things I could mention in my attempt to illustrate how these events are just dots that can and do affect our lives in ways that we don't connect together.

I must let you know that I have a great relationship with my parents. Even my biological father and I have developed a relationship that I am so amazed to have. My stepfather, who I have never seen as my stepfather, came into my life when I was two years old and I have always looked at him as my father. He raised me and did everything he was able to do to assure that my mom and I were taken care of. I Love him very much and am so grateful for the relationship God has allowed us to have.

One of my greatest fears is to lose my mind. I believe that is why I am so transparent about what is going on with me. I am so grateful to have at least one or two people in my life that are always willing to take my call. They have made it very clear that no matter what my fears are telling me, they never get tired of hearing from me. There is no reason for me not to call. If you are anything like me you may be able to relate to the fact that I believe I am a person who feels very deeply for others and sometimes it feels very not normal. But what I know is those feelings are good feelings and I have been running away from them all of my life. Why? Because I was always told that I trust too much, I love too much, I talk too much, I want to help people too much.

I want you to know I got sober on March 3, 1988 and am still sober today. The reason I believe God wanted me to talk about this is because if I had not started the process of removing one onion layer at a time, I would not be in a position to be used in the manner God had planned to use me. I am no longer asking is this God speaking to me…I know it's God!

So if you are trying to look the part or act the part it will be so much better and rewarding when you allow God to search your heart . . .because then He will reveal to you what's holding you back from accepting His love and blessings for. Once it's been identified our mentors won't have to work so hard because you will trust God's voice when you hear it rather than seeking out someone to confirm what you believe God is speaking to you! Set yourself free! Yank the rug up and expose everything under it to the Son… oh that just came out, I meant the sun.

IT'S NOT A SURPRISE TO GOD

For you formed my inward parts; you knitted me together in my mother's womb. I praise you, for I am fearfully and wonderfully made. Wonderful are your works; my soul knows it very well. My frame was not hidden from you, when I was being made in secret, intricately woven in the depths of the earth. Your eyes saw my unformed substance; in your book were written, every one of them, the days that were formed for me, when as yet there was none of them.

Nothing that happens in our lives is a surprise to God. He knew us before we were born - our personality, gifts, hang- ups, our potential, His plans for us, everything. To Him our lives are significant, important, and have dignity because we are created in His image. Whether you are the child of a President or the child of a prostitute your life is significant to God. Even in our sinfulness God is still there. His sanctifying work in the lives of each of us is a restoration process of His image in us. When we forget people are made in the image of God, dehumanization is bound to follow.

The entire ministry of Jesus was about finding value in the least the last and the lost. 1. Widow of Nain – He brings her son back to life 2. Woman caught in adultery – Rejected & condemned by others, He reaches out to the one & gives her acceptance, forgiveness, & another chance 3. Blind Bartimaeus – In the midst of a crowd along a dusty road, Jesus reaches out to the one and gives him His sight 4. Man living in the tombs – Rejected by others, Jesus reaches out to the one and delivers him from demon possession. Jesus cares about each and every one of us and teaches us that there is value even in the one.

LIVING AND LEARNING THROUGH LOSS

Denika Penn Carothers

The saying goes "what a difference a day makes." On June 8, 1999, I experienced the reality of this statement first hand.

My baby girl turned 4 years old on June 7, 1999. It was a day of celebration with cake and ice cream. My only sister was not able to attend the celebration so I put her cake aside and placed it in the refrigerator with the intention to give it to her the next day.

That night as I lay in my bed falling asleep after 12 midnight, I heard the cell phone of my now ex-husband vibrate. He thought I was asleep and grabbed for his phone to call his voice mail and retrieve the message. As he did, I discreetly watched his fingers on the lighted key pad as he dialed in his pass code. I pretended to get up to use the bathroom so I could write the code down.

As he showered the next morning, I used his pass code to retrieve his voice message, the one that had come in after midnight. To my surprise not one, but two messages played in my ear... female voices. The first message made my stomach sink "I love you and I miss you and I can't wait to see you again."

I broke into a cold sweat as I felt a wave of nausea come over me. Next message, "I appreciate the way you take care of me and I wanted to say thank you. I love you." As I felt the anger begin to rise, I had to sit down and process it.

I had my suspicions for a long time, but he was a well-practiced liar. However, there was no lying his way out of this one and I had a decision to make. The first decision I made was to remain calm. My children, then 10, 8 and 4, were in the house and I didn't want to start anything in front of them. I made myself busy with getting them ready for school. With one car at the time, it was necessary that we all ride together to get to school and work. The drive in was a very quiet one for me. I tuned everything out as I thought about what I needed to do.

Once the children were dropped off, I was then taken to work. As we pulled into the parking lot, he turned to me and asked if I was okay.

"No I am not okay, but I will be," I answered.

"What's wrong?" he asked

"What's wrong is you are a liar and a cheat and I am so grateful that God exposed you before I left my home and moved to another island with you." Even I was surprised at the calm in the tone of my voice.

We were making preparations to leave my home and relocate to another island so he could work. The "I love you and can't wait to see you again" woman was on this other island. Can you say with me "God Is GOOD!"

He looked at me with that shocked face. As he started to speak I stopped him.

"I heard your voice messages, so don't bother to try to feed me a story." I told him.

He HAD to explain himself. After expressing to me how much he loved me and how badly he wanted me and his family, he told me the best/worst lie I have ever been told. The explanation was that the "I love you and can't wait to see you again" message had been left by his cousin, who was trying to convince an admirer that she was in a relationship with someone. She decided to call his phone and pretend he was her boyfriend in front of said admirer.

The second explanation was that the second message was a prank call.

"How long is my tail and how big are my ears? Because you must think I'm the biggest jackass walking on two legs!" I shouted. My intelligence had been insulted and the calm had left the vehicle.

"Haven't you ever received prank calls?" he asked with this stupid dumbfounded look on his face.

As I shook my head and exited the car, I shouted, "We're done! It's over and you need to make plans to leave the house as soon as possible!"

I was in such a restless space that day. I remember not being able to sit still and got up from my desk to take an hour walk around the downtown area. When I got back to work I was told that my sister had called me. I called her back.

"You called me?" I asked as she answered the phone.

"Yeah, but I don't remember what I called you for," she replied.

"Well if you remember call me back." I didn't feel like talking and wanted to disconnect quickly. My sister and I were very close and she would sense my energy. I didn't feel like offering any explanations or talking about the situation yet, so I said goodbye and hung up the phone.

I was supposed to see her later that day, but I received a phone call from a friend of mine asking me if I would help him with Praise & Worship at a church that he had been asked to minister at last minute. He pleaded with me for my help and I agreed to help him out. Well as you can imagine, trying to sing praise and worship after my morning discovery was pretty difficult. But he was a good friend, who would not hesitate to help me if I called on him, so I made the effort.

That night after I took my shower, I heard the phone ringing in the kitchen. My ex-husband was at home but was in the bedroom and didn't hear the phone ringing. I got dressed and decided to check the answering machine before lying down. There was one message from a family friend. When I called her back, she informed me that she had just witnessed my sister being put into an ambulance and that she had been involved in a car accident.

I ran next door to my parents and informed them. We all drove to the hospital together, myself, my parents and my ex-husband. When we arrived we were told by the nursing staff that they were "working on her."

My sister's husband, who was at the hospital when we got there, came over to where we stood and told us that my sister had been in a car accident and she was in the emergency room. When we inquired as to her condition, he told us the same thing that the nurses had already told us. We were a well-known family living on a small island. One of the nurses on duty was one of our church sisters. She came over and told us that she would let us know as soon as she knew something.

I got that sinking feeling in my stomach again, much like the one I had experienced that morning when I listened to those voice messages. At that moment in my anxiety, the only thing that I was able to do was to pray. I told my family that we needed to pray so we all joined hands in a circle for prayer. As we prayed, I heard two songs in my spirit. For a long time Spirit communicated with me in and through songs.

The first song I heard was "It's Alright Now for I am in my Savior's Care" and right after that line was sung to me I heard the song "It is Well With my Soul".

"Oh no!" I shouted in my head. "Those are funeral songs! I am not singing those!"

After we finished praying my mother and I were standing off to the side and my father came over to us.

"I just heard 'Kris is not going to fight'", he said as he looked at both of us with a heaviness in his face.

This made my mother furious. "What do you mean she's not going to fight? Of course she's going to fight! She's going to fight for us and for her son

Navah!" Her tone was one of irritation, anger, fear and nervousness.

Very humbly my father responded, "That's what I heard."

I did not tell them about the songs I heard during our prayer.

The next thing I remember is the doctor coming over to us and asking us to please follow her, as she led us into a room. I wanted to vomit. I wanted to pass out. I knew it before she even said it. My entire body began to vibrate.

"I'm sorry, we did everything we could. Kristin did not make it."

My mother collapsed into my father's arms as she let out a loud scream, and my brother n' law went down to the floor as my ex-husband went over to console him.

"I need to go to her!" I said as I looked straight into the doctor's eyes.

"I'm sorry but you can't go right now." She replied.

"I need to go to her NOW!" I shouted at her as I made my way to the door.

I don't know who he was, but a man tried to step in front of me as I made my way past him towards the door. I heard voices behind me saying "let her go."

As I entered into the emergency room and saw my sister's dead body lying on the table I can't explain the feeling that I was experiencing. All I knew in that moment was that I needed to pray over her body.

As I stood over her with my hands running up and down her arms I began to thank God for her life, for the 29 years that I was allowed to have her as my sister. As I prayed I committed her soul and spirit back to God. And then I caught myself, or more specifically my flesh caught up with what was happening and decided to take over.

"What the hell are you doing?" I asked myself. "You are standing over your sister's dead body saying thank you for the 29 years you HAD her. You no longer HAVE her! She's gone!"

As I was having this inner dialogue with myself, I noticed people starting to come into the room. Mummy wailing, daddy sobbing with a look of disbelief and utter pain on his face, my brother n' law down on his knees on the floor next to her body, my brother n' law's sister standing there just shaking her head from side to side.

Then I felt it. It started at my feet and made its way up to my throat. A shrilling scream that could probably break glass came out of my mouth. I stormed out of the room, screaming as I walked down the hospital hallway. My priest came up to me and put his arms around me to hold me.

"Let me go!" I screamed at him. "Don't touch me!" I shouted as I went down to the floor. A nurse came over to help me up. The same nurse who had tended to me in the hospital 3 weeks earlier when I was admitted for a 3rd degree burn that I had received on my left thigh. She reminded me about my leg as she pleaded with me to get up off of the floor.

The pain in my heart was so great, that in that moment, I was not even aware of the pain in my leg. Nothing I had ever felt in my life up to that point, felt as painful as what I felt in that moment. Up until this moment I would have told you that the debridement of the burned leg 3 weeks earlier was the worst pain I had ever felt. It didn't even come close to the pain that I felt in that moment.

I remember after they had put my only sister's body in the morgue, we asked to go in and be with her. There were quite a few family members standing around her body. I lay my head down on my sister's stomach as I sang Yolanda Adam's

'There is No Pain Jesus Can't Feel, no hurt He cannot heal.

For all things work according to His Holy will

No matter what, you're going through

Remember God is using you.

For the battle is not yours, it's the Lord's" As I sang, my aunt stroked my hair and said "Sing baby. Sing Nika, sing."

When I had finished, I looked around and noticed that my father was not there.

"Where's daddy?" I asked

"The doctors are working on him." My ex-husband answered.

"Working on him for what?" My nerves started to rise again. "Where is he?"

"He's in the emergency room. I think something is wrong with his heart." He replied.

I looked to mummy for answers but she was overtaken in grief as she rubbed the body of her baby girl lying there in the morgue.

I left to go see about my daddy. As I entered into the emergency room, I saw that they had him hooked up to a heart monitor. When I inquired what was happening, I was told that they needed to keep him in for observation. My father had never had any issues with his heart before this.

As we left the hospital, my sister in the morgue and my father in the emergency room, my mother and I walked hand in hand to the car. We got in the back seat together and my ex-husband drove. My mother laid her head in my lap. As I stroked her hair all I remember her saying through her tears is "Oh Nika, Kris is gone, Kris is gone."

My mother who had all my life been a source of strength for me, now needed me to be a source of strength for her. I made a decision that I would process my grief as I needed to, but that I needed to be there for my mummy now. As we got back home I took her up to her bedroom, tucked her into her bed and got in beside her. As a steady stream of tears rolled down my cheeks, I held my mother in my arms until she fell asleep.

The next morning as we both awoke, to what we realized was not a bad dream, the tears began to flow again. Shortly after we woke the hospital called to say that we could come and pick daddy up. Being the only daughter, now the only child, I decided that I needed to go and get my daddy. I needed to be sure that he was okay.

As I drove, I thought about how I had experienced a double whammy in one day. In the morning I told my ex-husband it was over... my marriage was gone. In the night my sister was killed in a car accident... my sister was gone. I had just experienced two major losses in one day. Two days ago I was celebrating life and on June 9th, 1999 I was grieving, my heart was broken by two major events and my life had completely changed. I was now my mother's only living child. I was a husbandless wife. I was a single mother. I didn't know how my heart was going to heal from this. I didn't know how I was going to move forward with all this pain.

I had the most surreal experience as I drove to the hospital, in my thoughts, the day after my sister died, to pick my father up. I began to notice life around me. I noticed the birds flying. I noticed the sun shining. I noticed people driving in their cars. I noticed people walking, talking and laughing. I noticed life was still happening. Life continued to exist. Here I was having the worst moment of my life, yet life had not stopped. I was still living. I realized in that moment, while driving the car, that I had two choices before me. I could either, curl up and die as I felt I wanted to, or I could make a decision to live through this and live in spite of this.

I had a mother who loved me and who I had to be there for. I had children who I loved more than anything, who needed me, who I needed to help understand this life changing event. I had friends who were standing with me and loving me in this. I had a church family who was praying for me. And I realized in that moment that I had a Creator God who was with me, who promised me that I would never have to go through more than I could bare. A God who promised me that He would never leave me or forsake me, and that His strength was made perfect in my time of weakness! I focused on what I HAD, yes my sister was no longer here, and my marriage was over, but there was so much that I still did have.

I found strength in this realization that I cannot explain. As I write this I feel that same strength. I learned that I had access to strength even when I did not feel strong. I learned that I could live, even when I wanted to die. I learned that our loved ones never leave us. They change forms, but they don't cease to exist. I learned that in every experience there are individual lessons that we are to learn; that every experience comes to teach us something.

What I learned in my experience the day that my sister passed and my marriage ended was, first and foremost, that no matter what comes my way God has me in the palm of His hand. I learned that we never know what we can bare, until we have to bare it. My sister and I were extremely close. She was my baby sister, and she was one of my best friends (my mother was my other best friend). I never would have believed that I could make it through her passing, and many days I wasn't sure that I would. But I did and I am here, and able to now share it with others with the hope and prayer that I am able to offer strength and encouragement to someone else because I survived this experience.

I learned that people come into your life for a season and a reason and that when those reasons have been fulfilled and the season is over, that it's okay to release it to the wind and move on to the next relationship or experience. I learned that what we go through is not for us alone. I learned that every test ushers in a testimony and that in every messed up situation, there is a message.

I learned that the power of life and death truly does lie in the tongue. I learned that I create my reality based on what I think, what I believe, and what I say. I learned that who God keeps is well kept. I learned that I can truly do ALL things through the power of Christ, wherein I find my strength and my comfort. I learned that God is true to His word and that if I hold to the unchanging love and compassion of God, I will always be okay, no matter what trial or tribulation I have to face.

I learned that life throws us curve balls, that we don't expect, but that we can overcome every situation of adversity, that we can catch those balls or we can duck so that they don't hit us and knock us out. I learned that, like Kenny Rogers says, you gotta know when to hold em and know when to fold em. I learned that God is able to keep me, even when I may feel that I don't want to be kept.

I learned that life is a gift that can and should be unwrapped every day. I learned that the only person who is responsible for my experiences, my feelings and my thoughts is me. I learned that I can choose to see the glass half full and not half empty. I learned that power does not reside outside of me, but my power is within me. I learned that I CAN create my reality. I learned that I CAN be happy, that I CAN be grateful and that I CAN have the desires of my heart.

I learned that all things do work together for the good to them that love the Lord. I learned that there is PURPOSE in everything. I learned that I am here for a reason and that I am able to fulfill my purpose. I learned that we are all connected one to another, and that there really is no separation other than the separation in our minds.

I learned that LOVE truly conquers all and that if I am not living from a place of love I am living from a place of fear, and that I can choose not to operate from a fear place. I learned that the spirit that is my birthright from God is one of Love, Light and Power. I learned that I AM whatever I acknowledge, believe and confess that I am.

I learned that I am an over-comer, a warrior and a strong and mighty woman. I learned that being good and kind to people will take you further than any position or title will. I learned that what I give to others, I will receive. I learned to never sow a seed that I would not want to eat the fruit of. I learned that gratitude ushers in the blessings of God.

I learned to BE the hands, feet and heart of God in the earth. I learned that LOVE conquers all, Love NEVER fails and that Love never leaves us if we welcome it to stay. I learned that I can learn through loss and that I can live through loss.

I learned Who I am, Why I AM and Whose I am and I am grateful for all the lessons.

HEALING THE BROKENHEARTED

He healeth the broken in heart, and bindeth up their wounds. Psalm 147:3 KJV

How does God heal? Part of the healing process involves changing the way we think about ourselves? Look at a verse from Romans

"Do not be conformed to this world, but be transformed by the renewing of your mind, that you may prove what is that good and acceptable and perfect will of God." Romans 12:2 (NKJV)

The Bible places great emphases on our thought life. Our thoughts are powerful. They direct our lives. Proverbs tells us:

"As a man thinks in his heart, so he is." Proverbs 23:7. If you view yourself as a loser you're going to tend to be a loser in life. If you view yourself as a failure, you're going to tend to fail. But if you see yourself as a winner – you will give more effort to winning. If you see yourself as an over-comer – you will put more effort into overcoming. It's very simple – our beliefs determine our behaviors. The way we think determines the way that we act – therefore we ought to think in a manner which pleases God.

All of us are fearfully and wonderfully made. God created us to be unique. He knows every hair on our heads. He knew that our finger prints were going to be different. He knew that our personalities would be different. He knows the exact moment that we were born and He knows the exact moment that we will die. He knows our thoughts and our motives. He knows us inside and out. Yes – we are all human – but we are all also unique and that makes each and every one of us valuable. We are each one of a kind – created in God's image. We have value. We have worth. We were bought with a price. You may ask what price? I can tell you. Jesus gave His life for you. Jesus came to heal you. He came to make you well. He came to save you. He went to a cross to die for your sins – in order that you do not have to die for them yourself. He paid the price – He suffered the punishment – in order that we do not have to suffer the punishment ourselves.

We are loved by God unconditionally even in the midst of our hurt, even in the midst of our pain. When we recognize that beyond a shadow of a doubt the healing can begin.

Mother is a Verb

Cheryl Lacey Donovan

It's been several years since I wrote "The Ministry of Motherhood" It was in that book that I coined the phrase, *Mother is a verb. It's something you do not just who you are.* Since then it has circulated on several blogs, websites, and social media outlets. But that phrase never became more meaningful than it is right now.

Being a mother has been one of the most rewarding things I have ever done. I tried to the best of my ability to be a faithful steward over the lives I had been given to nurture. But sometimes even your best is not enough to protect your children for the dangers lurking around every corner.

It was about 5 years ago now that I learned my youngest son was using prescription drugs; Xanax to be exact. I had noticed that he sometimes seemed to be extremely lethargic but like most parents I didn't want to believe what I was seeing.

One Saturday evening my son and my husband's cousin were standing in front of our home. I heard loud voices coming from the front yard so I immediately sprang to my feet and rushed to the front door to see what was happening. To my utter dismay a police car was in front of my home and the officers were arresting my son for marijuana possession.

Now I must be honest and say that the first thoughts that went through my mind were about others I knew who had used marijuana for years and never got caught. How could this be happening? Why was my son the one? However, the spirit of God soon revealed to me why it had to happen this way. You see, had this one event never taken place, I may never have known about the prescription drug use which was far more detrimental to my son's health and wellbeing.

After his arrest my son was taken to the city jail and ultimately transferred to the county because of traffic tickets that had not been paid. This was one of the most devastatingly horrible nights I had ever experienced because for the first time in his life I had no idea where my son was and I was unable to do anything about it. My son spent several days in the county jail before being released. What I saw when I was finally able to lay eyes on him was something that in my mind most assuredly was out of some terrible nightmare I was having. He was disheveled, unkempt, and a little off balance. I had to pick him up from a nearby church because he was so out of it the police clerk noticed and said if he didn't leave their campus they were going to re arrest him. Because of the bruising on his face I assumed he had been beaten or otherwise hurt in jail. I later learned he had suffered a seizure in jail. This had never happened before but as the events unfolded I would soon learn why.

I took my son home but he just didn't seem right. He took a shower and ate dinner but he was very anxious and unsure. Before the evening was over his episode escalated into a full blown disconnect with reality. He was asking questions that made no sense and wandering around the house like he had no idea where he was.

Distraught and unsure of what to do, my husband and I took him to the local hospital emergency room. However, this proved to be useless because in their eyes his condition wasn't bad enough to be seen right away. Increasingly belligerent and agitated my son stormed out of the hospital and into the cold dark streets. I literally ran after him and peed my pants because I was so afraid that he would be arrested again for disorderly conduct or something worse. Needless to say all I could do was pray that God would intervene.

After much coercing, police intervention, and yes prayer, we were able to get my son into our vehicle so we could take him home. He was insistent about leaving the house in this state of mind. He was angry that we wouldn't let him go. I knew in my heart of hearts that if I allowed him to get passed me and go into the streets it would end badly. No one out there would know what was going on and might misconstrue his intentions. In his anger he tried to pour water on my husband who seemed to bear the brunt of my son's anger. Maybe because he was the one who demanded that he be responsible and accountable for his actions. But he didn't deserve this. His attentions diverted to me as he tried to move me from the front door. When he looked at me I didn't recognize him at all. I saw nothing in his eyes that even resembled him. Yet, there was something else about him that was begging me to tell him what was happening. It was as if he didn't really understand what he had done to himself or to me. I thought my son was dying. I thought that that was my last moment with him. I thought it was over.

It would be another thirty-six hours of behaving violently, ranting and raving, threats, and psychotic behavior before I would finally get up the courage to call the mental health police unit to take my son away in an ambulance kicking and screaming. Upon their arrival my son tried to break through a window and was rolling in the floor naked. He spit on the officers and tried to bite one of them. He later shared with me that the officer who had come for him looked like devils. The amazing thing about this experience is when we read scripture to him it seemed to calm him.

My oldest son and sister decided it was best for me to stay at home and rest after the thirty-six hour ordeal. They set up a watch at the hospital and refused to leave until everything possible had been done to determine what had just happened. We were all blindsided. We had never been through anything like this before. For the first time in my life I was unsure what to do or say. I didn't have an answer to give anyone. No words of encouragement that it would be ok. The only one who could intervene in this situation was God.

After staying in the hospital for a week we learned that he had been using Xanax, a prescription drug that obviously had not been prescribed for him. Even the doctors were confounded at how he had responded. But the reality was he had gone cold turkey from the prescription drugs and marijuana. All of this had been a full blown detox from the drugs.

You would think this experience would have been enough for him to stay away from drugs forever. Nevertheless, fast forward two years and we find ourselves in nearly the same place. However, this time, it is because of synthetic marijuana. You see, my son surmised that using this synthetic drug would be different, it would be better because it was "legal" at the time. Not only was it legal but drug tests would come back normal because there were no tests for the drugs used in this mixture.

Synthetic marijuana is cheap, readily available at convenience stores nationwide, and is leaving a trail of dead and severely injured users in its wake, making it one of the most alarming new drugs available anywhere, according to medical experts and drug enforcement officials.

Synthetic marijuana is often sold as incense or potpourri, and can be branded with many names. The substance is a mixture of various herbs, sprayed with an assortment of chemicals whose effects purportedly mimic the high from regular marijuana when smoked.

Synthetic marijuana was declared illegal in July 2012 after President Barack Obama signed legislation that banned five of the chemicals commonly used to make it. But manufacturers have avoided the ban by using different chemicals in their mixture, which adds to the dangers of the drug. Adverse effects can be lethal and some experts say could include permanent brain damage. Side effects may include "agitation, vomiting, hallucination, paranoia, tremor, seizure, tachycardia, hypokalemia, chest pain, cardiac problems, stroke, kidney damage, acute psychosis, brain damage and death," according to Forbes.

This bout with synthetic marijuana had him talking 90 MPH and his thoughts were racing all over the place. He talked about the 'truths' he had discovered and his need to get the 'truth' to as many people as possible. He felt that this was his purpose in this life. He thought he was God. As I sat listening to him babbling on and on, my mind was racing, trying to figure out what to do. Eventually I decided to call my older son, Christian and ask him to come over and help me decide how to handle the situation.

I called the psychiatric Center and they advised me to take him in for an assessment or call the police and ask them to come and do a Safety Check on him. If they determined that he was a danger to himself or others, they would be able to take him by force for an assessment.

Neither option set very well with me. I honestly didn't think I could convince him to go with me to the hospital. I was afraid he'd get upset and leave. On the other hand, I couldn't stomach the idea of him being dragged away yet again.

However, because his blood pressure was now elevated I decided to call the mental health unit. Police officers arrived at our door and after assessing him decided to call an ambulance to transport him to the psychiatric center. While in the waiting area my son felt compelled to go there to help 'someone' learn the 'truth'. None of the people seemed to be interested in the help he was offering. The center diagnosed him as bi-polar. During this time I walked around with a rock in my stomach every day, afraid that something else would happen.

Sitting here now, I have no idea how this will continue to affect our lives. It's quite possible my son will need care giving his entire life, or he may be blessed to excel in spite of being Bi-Polar. Whatever the case I know God is with me.

So, what did I learn from all this? First, I learned I was enabling my son, because so much of the time I was just trying to keep the peace. Tough love is sometimes tough to do. Because of everything else going on in my life it was just easier to lighten up. But as his issues became more severe, I had no choice but to figure out how to do tough love right and stick with it. At one point this left my son temporarily homeless, because it became apparent the drug was more important to him than his family. He didn't want to stay in a rehab center. That was hard to do because the implications of doing something like tossing your child out of your house, has the potential for serious consequences. I learned to make peace with the decision and have been working on taking care of myself so I can be stronger for whatever lies ahead. The separation has been tough because He and I have always shared a very close relationship. The disconnect in our relationship, part of Bipolar, has been especially hard to adjust to.

Today he is doing better at least for now. He holds a seasonal job, but he still has residual effects from the drugs he's taking. Many have said He's a drug addict and I just need to come to grips with that. Others have said I should just give up on him. Still others don't understand my dogged tenacity to believe that God is still in control and that all things will work together for our good. My response, God doesn't give up on me-period. I am His daughter and I know that all that I do does not always please Him. Yet, each and every day I wake up to new mercies. Nothing separates me from His love and nothing will separate my son from mine.

During this entire ordeal the one thing that consistently resonated in my spirit was that all their lives (he has an older brother), in my attempts to be a faithful steward, I had done more than that, I had become their god. I was the one they turned to when things went wrong. I was the one they turned to when they were in trouble. I was the one who cleaned up all the messes and mistakes.

One day God spoke to me in a still small voice and said, "Daughter If you continue to be the one who saves them, then there is no room for me." Wow what an epiphany. I had never thought of it that way before. I was standing in the way of what God wanted for their lives. I was standing in the way of my son's ability to seek God because he always came to me first. Unfortunately, I don't get a 'do over', I can only do better from here forward.

While we may not be out of the woods yet, I believe God. He is faithful and He is able. He knows the plans He has for my son and those plans are to prosper him and give him an expected end. I have learned to truly cast my care on Him and trust His plans concerning my son's life. Most importantly I have learned I can no longer be his god.

WITH ARMS WIDE OPEN

...And when he came to himself...Luke 15:17 KJV

...For this my son was dead, and is alive again; he was lost, and is found. And they began to be merry. Luke 15:24 KJV

Each of us at some point in our lives have found ourselves outside the will of God. We've found ourselves either doing things He has told us not to do. Or not doing things that He told us to do. We've all felt at one time or another that we knew what was best for our lives and totally ignored the Lord on our decisions. We've felt like we had it going on and didn't need Him for anything. We went about our own way in the world doing what we wanted to do, when we wanted to it and how we wanted to do it. And once we found ourselves dealing with the consequences of our defiance we remember that we have a Father to go to in the time of our trouble. Unlike some earthly fathers, this Father is always standing there with His arms wide open waiting patiently for us to come to ourselves. Loving us unconditionally in spite of ourselves. Nothing, not even our own rebellion can separate us from the love of this Father; our Father.

Isn't it good news that when we mess up He's right there to help us clean up?

REFLECTIONS

I AM BLESSED

I know that I am blessed. I remind myself to be content with what I have. I cultivate a sense of gratitude and thank others for their kindness.

I share my riches with others. I pitch in when a coworker is swamped and take time to listen when a friend is going through a difficult time. I volunteer in my community and extend my hospitality to newcomers and old friends.

I keep my attention focused on the good things in my life. I avoid fretting about past disappointments or comparing myself to others. I realize that I have all that I need to be happy in this present moment.

I acknowledge my potential and accomplishments. Thinking about my victories builds my confidence and inspires me to aim higher.

I treasure my health and wellbeing. With a strong body and sound mind, I can take on challenges and fulfill my dreams.

I value my family and friends. I let them know that they are a vital part of my life.

I appreciate my education, and the opportunity to do meaningful work. My knowledge, wisdom, and skills help me to contribute to society and provide for my family.

I enjoy the beauty that surrounds me. I take a walk around my neighborhood to marvel at nature and renew my energy. I listen to music that eases my tension and cheers me up.

Today, I count my blessings. I treat each day as a precious gift.

DISCUSSION QUESTIONS

1. How can I spot blessings that initially look like hardships?

2. What is one blessing that I tend to take for granted?

3. How does counting my blessings attract more happiness and good fortune?

I FIND SOLACE IN PRAYING

Praying brings me serenity, peace, and optimism that all things always work out for the best. To me, they are a beautiful way to communicate with my Creator. I make it a point to pray often so I can stay in touch with my soul and Creator.

I am proud to pray on a regular basis.

I pray each day because it gives me great comfort to put my thoughts up to my Creator. This comfort is a blessing that I can receive whenever I want.

My spouse and I pray together and we find it to be a joy for both of us. We also teach our children to pray on a regular basis so they can enjoy the graces it gives to them. They love to pray with us, and we hope they continue praying as they mature.

I pray with my friends and community. Together, we offer up prayers and songs for worship.

We ask for forgiveness for straying from our values, express gratitude for our blessings, and request whatever help we need for our families.

Praying together strengthens my bond with my family and community. Praying together provides some of the best quality times that we spend together.

Today, I find comfort in praying by myself and with my family, friends, and neighbors.

DISCUSSION QUESTIONS

1.   How can I use prayer to enhance my
     life?

2.   In what ways can prayer heighten my
     spiritual journey?

3.   What can I do to encourage praying
     with my family and friends?

I FORGIVE MYSELF FOR RELATIONSHIP MISTAKES

I let go of my errors with past relationships. I have learned what I can from my missteps and refuse to allow regrets to take up space in my mind or spirit.

I accept my mistakes without guilt or embarrassment.

I understand the universe presents a variety of experiences to strengthen the spirit, and mistakes are a natural part of the learning curve.

My past relationship errors help me identify my current values. They clarify what I am looking for in a relationship and how I can better meet my partner's needs. I now understand how my actions and words can affect others and am conscientious about my communications.

I am able to heal emotionally after my relationship mistakes. I am also able to help others heal by being an example for them.

My perception of past relationships is clear and I am able to embrace new relationships with ease. I look upon my mistakes of the past as blessings in disguise and know how to nurture positive elements in my relationships going forward.

Today, I leave the past in the past and look forward to a bright future with positive, fulfilling relationships.

DISCUSSION QUESTIONS

1. How can I stop my mind from focusing on my past relationships?

2. How can I learn from my relationship errors and move forward to new, positive relationships?

3. What can I do to help my friends to move past their relationship mistakes?

I RELEASE RESENTMENT IN MY HEART

I give myself the gift of freedom from resentment. I let go of anger, forgive others, and make room for love.

I dig deep into my soul to discover why resentment accumulates in my heart. I find the source of my resentment so I can let it go. I refuse to allow the pain of resentment to fester inside me. I learn strategies that I can use to release negative emotions in a healthy way and I practice them daily.

I am able to block resentment from feeding on my thoughts and feelings. I release it back into the universe and replace it with positive thoughts.

I understand the power of resentment and its ability to harm my mind and body.

To help me let go of resentment, I study positive communication methods. I understand how to discuss my feelings. I can express my emotions with confidence. My relationships remain secure while I express my thoughts.

I can also let go of bitterness because I understand that my past can only affect my present or future if I let it. My choice is to learn what I can from unfortunate situations, leave them in the past, and move forward without them.

Today, I gladly let go of any resentment in my heart and move forward toward a happy life without this negative emotion.

DISCUSSION QUESTIONS

1. How can I learn to forgive others? Why would I want to?

2. What can I do to release the resentment I feel toward those who hurt me?

3. How can I prevent anger from consuming my spirit?

THE DOOR IS HALF OPEN

Optimism is perception. When I view the world with a positive attitude, good things happen. I see more opportunity. More doors are open to me.

Because I see the door as half open, I perceive it as opening instead of closing. It is a simple, positive decision. I see expanding potential and seize the ability to progress—to move forward through the open door.

I begin to view everything in this manner. The glass is half full, tasks are almost done. Each day, I move closer to my goals. Mountains appear smaller, and rivers narrower. I relish new challenges because obstacles are meant to be overcome.

My perception, in turn, affects those around me. Instead of letting the door close, I hold it open for others. I encourage them to view opportunities in a new, positive light.

Every open door is an opportunity, regardless of how much it is open.

Challenges are like doors. When I find myself in front of a closed door, I am certain that I can figure out how to open it. If the door is locked, I search for the key. Maybe I have the key. Sometimes, I need to ask others for the key.

Today, I perceive everything with a positive attitude. Each task, opportunity, or challenge is a door half open, and it is up to me to walk through.

DISCUSSION QUESTIONS

1. How do I overcome negative perceptions (both mine and those of others)?

2. Who inspires me to think positive?

3. How can I inspire others to be optimistic?

ACCOUNTABILITY EQUALS DEPENDABILITY

Everyone makes mistakes. When I make a mistake, I own it. I learn from the error and am bettered by it.

I accept accountability for my decisions and actions. Being responsible is a way of being and thinking for me. It empowers me, because I feel increased control over events in my life.

I take equal pride in my strengths and shortcomings. I refrain from making excuses. Instead, I develop resolutions. Resolutions are an acknowledgement of the challenges I face, coupled with a solution for overcoming.

For others, it may be easier to be irresponsible. Being accountable is demanding, but I rise to the occasion. I police my own actions because I have a responsibility to myself. I must be able to depend on myself before others can.

When I voice responsibility for my actions, others notice. I am an example for them to follow because I am reliable and trustworthy. They know they can depend on me. Because I am dependable, my decisions and actions affect and influence theirs.

Persistence, honesty, and integrity are fundamental traits I possess. I rely on these traits when I accept accountability for shortcomings.

Today, my ability to accept responsibility has a positive impact on others. I am looked to for guidance. I seek new ways to guide others. It feels great to know others can rely on me to help them overcome obstacles.

DISCUSSION QUESTIONS

1. Whom do I look to for guidance?

2. How has being accountable had a positive impact in my life?

3. Have I seen examples of the adverse effects of being irresponsible?

I LIVE AN AUTHENTIC LIFE

I live my life according to my own principles. The outside world has very little impact on my choices. I am proud to be true to myself and have a strong sense of purpose.

My beliefs drive each decision I make in my personal and professional life. I avoid using the appeal of success to sway my mindset.

I enjoy gaining recognition at work for a job well done. But I am happier to gain that reward because I work in a principled manner. My mission is always to do well while staying true to myself.

Friends know that I am the real deal. The person I am with my friends is the person I am at all times. They appreciate that I am honest.

My views on their actions are directly tied to my values. Even though I am gentle when giving advice, I avoid compromising my views to make others feel better. I prefer to be honest than to say what someone wants to hear. It is authentic to be truthful.

Today, my peace of mind comes from living an authentic life. I commit to remaining true to myself and being honest with others. Each day is a chance to renew that commitment.

DISCUSSION QUESTIONS

1. How do I respond to others who want me to create a false impression?

2. How quickly do I recognize when a situation is testing my authenticity?

3. What activities can help me to maintain focus on living according to the real me?

ABOUT THE
AUTHORS

OLEVIA HENDERSON

Olevia Henderson was born and raised in Shreveport, Louisiana. She currently resides in Houston, TX. She is the mother of 7; five daughters and two sons. She is the grandmother of one. She recently signed with Imani Faith Publishing so she adds Author to her bio. She is also a motivational speaker and life coach. Olevia is walking in her calling and vision that God gave her as Founder of Rebuilt Ministry where her mission is to bring others into the Kingdom under God's teaching. She is the owner of her own business; Texas Legal Ease where she provides multiple services from (tax preparer, process server, certified notary signing agent). She is the former chapter president of Survivor's With Voice's Foundation. She is a mighty Woman of God who loves giving back and encouraging and empowering others. Most of all she is a survivor of abuse on all levels yet her faith in God never wavered. As a single mom and divorced woman she was still able to become Founder and Director of an Anti – Bullying Foundation known as HABB (Healing After Being Bullied) formerly known as B.E.N.(Bullying Ends Now). Olevia lives to spread God's word and help others.

CEE CEE H. CALDWELL – MILLER

Cee Cee H. Caldwell- Miller is a native of Washington, DC and she now resides in Plainfield, New Jersey. Cee Cee has had a love for writing since she was 5 years old when her mother use to tell her to go write a story to get rid of her. Cee Cee began writing poetry, then she moved to writing one act plays, then into article/blog writing and finally to book writing. She believes that everyone has a story to tell. Her love for the written and spoken word has increased as the years have gone by. In 2008, Cee Cee released her 1st book titled Be in Good Health: Living a Life of Happiness, Wholeness and Wellness which endeavors to help people live their best life, from the inside out in the 8 dimensions of wellness. Cee Cee released Unspoken Words "Love" Vol. I in October 2014 and has co-authored Network to Increase Your Net Worth in 2013 and Tainted Elegance in 2014.

Cee Cee speaks and facilitates workshops on the following topics: Being A Healthier U (Living Your

Best Life From The Inside Out), The ABC's of Business Basics, Success Principles, Passion and Purpose, Authentic Living, Wellness In The Workplace, Time Management (Whose Time is it Anyway) and The Art of Relaxing, Relating and Releasing, Kingdom Stewardship and Servant Leadership just to name a few. She has helped many people on their journey to reach and attain BUSINESS & PERSONAL SUCCESS and WELLNESS in their lives.

Cee Cee's favorite scripture is "I can do ALL things through Christ who strengthens me!" Cee Cee believes that "You must READ to SUCCEED, because Readers are Leaders!" Cee Cee's plans are to start a women's theatrical ensemble, a youth entrepreneurship program for teenage girls, a humanitarian foundation and restoration center in the future. Through her speaking, workshops and books she hopes to Encourage, Enlighten and Empower others to walk in their Greatness by living an Authentic and Intentional Life ON PURPOSE!

CLARA L. PETERS

Clara Peters is a pastor, radio talk show host, motivational speaker, mentor, certified life coach, blogger, and author. A woman of integrity.

Clara's first book will be published by Imani Faith Publishing in the winter of 2016

NICOLETTE HINES

Nicolette Hines has grown to be an amazing, Wife, Mother, Inspirational Speaker, Author and Lady in general. Through the gruesome trials of a dysfunctional childhood that subjected her to multiple trauma, confusion, sexual violation and a whirlwind of dramatic experiences; she survived. Those experiences exposed her to a lifestyle of teenage prostitution, left her in fear, introduced her to domestic violence, forced her to hide behind alcohol, robbed her of self-esteem, and tarnished her sense of moral quality and poise. Nicolette discovered great gifts inside of her after she was able to overhaul the pain of her past and work the process of deliverance. One of those gifts includes the ability to draw in which she is the artist that drew the Satisfied Woman on the cover of this awesome book. Who knows what lies beneath our pain? Nicolette will expose the scheme of the enemy to rob every woman of her moment of excellence and true Satisfaction. She has escaped the ruins of domestic violence, conquered the challenges of molestation, survived the decisions to lower her standards and recovered all including her pearls which are symbolic to her dignity.

LETISHA GALLOWAY

Letisha Galloway is from Woodstown, New Jersey and currently resides in Delaware. She obtained a Bachelor of Science degree in Criminal Justice from Wilmington University. She obtained a Master of Science degree in Administration of Human Services from Wilmington University. Ms. Galloway is presently a Senior Social Worker/Case Manager in Delaware.

Letisha is a poet, author, and speaker. Letisha is regularly involved in bringing awareness to domestic violence. Surviving domestic violence herself, she is a strong advocate for change and protection for those who feel they have no voice. Letisha is active in child abuse prevention activities.

Letisha is the mother of one, a son she named Jordan who is resting peacefully in the arms of Jesus.

RAMONA PEARCEY BURNETT

I grew up in Killeen, Fort Hood. My father served in the military for 30 years, so I was what they call a military brat. My family is pretty big – five boys and one girl. My mother, passed away from cancer when I was nine years old. My father raised me and my 5 brothers on his own after my mother passed. I am close to my family and talk to them daily. My husband, Anthony and I recently adopted the love our lives Lamona Jewel. I am stepmom to Tamika and Grandma Mona to Morgan. We also have 3 four legged babies Leo, Aries and Gemini!

Losing my mother at such an early age made me curious about the family structure. I always knew our family was different, given we lost my mom so early. I now understand that different is more than okay! We had the main component - LOVE. I enjoy discussing family matters and being a source of help and prayer for families under attack or in need of help.

I am passionate about being the best wife and mother I can be. I have been married for 7 years and have concluded that being a Christian and a wife, does not automatically make you a Christian Wife. You do not get the badge of Proverbs 31 at the altar! Marriage is a beautiful gift from God, but we have to do our part. I have learned much in my 7 years and endeavor to learn even more. I pray my writing will provide insight and help to women of all ages on their own journey – The Wife Journey.

SHAMARIAN BRADLEY

Minister Shamarian D. Bradley or "Minister Shaye" as she is known was licensed to preach the gospel by the Antioch Missionary Baptist Church in Beaumont, Texas under the Pastoral leadership of Dr. John R. Adolph, where she continues to serve as an Associate Minister. Minister Bradley is a powerful woman of God who with grace, has been tried, tested, elected and selected by God to declare and demonstrate the Power of the Word.

Minister Bradley is blessed as the founder of "Ladies Living for the Lord" a ministry that speaks to the hearts of women through prayer, testimony and most importantly Gods word. With compassion and understanding Minister Bradley serves as a Chaplain with the La Porte Police Department. Minister Bradley is a co-host for Real Life Real Faith Christian talk show where she serves alongside a phenomenal group of women.

Minister Bradley has just recently signed with Imani Faith Publishing as a new and upcoming author and she is determined to be whatever God wants her to be. It is her heartfelt desire to do everything she can to please God in every aspect of ministry that He calls her to do.

ESTHER RENEE WRIGHT

Esther Renee' Wright is a woman who is after God's heart and, is always on a mission to spread God's word. She is a teacher of the gospel, a chemical dependency counselor who absolutely loves assisting others with life issues.

She is the founder of Titus Works, Ministries, a vision she believes was downloaded specifically to her from God. This ministry has been created to spread the word freely to God's people. Titus based on the Word of God in Titus chapter 2, teaches us that the old shall be there to guide the young into a better life with Christ. This ministry strives to do this in a unique way. That through telephone empowerment conference calls, Esther Renee' with powerful speakers and topics is keeping it real with people and God.

Renee', has been blessed to counsel, motivate, inspire and encourage others that they too can be a living testimony. She is a humble servant that exemplifies an attitude of gratitude. She will tell you, "I AM GRATEFUL FOR EVERYTHING."

With all of that said the most important thing she would like for you to know about her, is she loves God with all of her heart and wants nothing more than for God to be pleased with everything she does.

DENIKA CAROTHERS

A native from the island of the Bahamas, Denika Carothers, a Mindset Transformation Coach, specializes in helping women, young and old, transform their mindset from one that is conflicting and limiting, to one that is empowering and liberating.

"Women are the heart of God in the earth, so they have to get their mindset in alignment with their heart space, in order to nurture the earth back to a healthy state." Denika Carothers

Her platform, C.H.A.N.G.E. – The Catalyst for Success, is designed to invigorate, inspire and provoke her audience to step out of their comfort zone, establish soulful connections, and live in their truth and power. With the gift of insight, she is able to tap into the heart and soul of others, as she helps them to identify the barriers in their life that cause emotional, mental and even spiritual conflicts.

Her passion for helping mothers to effectively connect with their children on a soulful level, comes from her own Soulful Connection experience with her children. She proudly boasts of having raised 3 amazing children, as a single mother, into successful adults. And while she would be the first to admit that it's not easy, she shows you how it is very possible and the amazing rewards that come with such a connection.

Her inspirational and life changing perspective, which she arrived at by conquering her own life challenges, offers her clients and audiences a transformational view of how to 'GROW' through their challenges and inner conflicts. Her clients and colleagues say that she is the "bridge between your questions and your answers."

She is an Empowerment and Motivational Speaker and Author. Her newest book, "Who in The Hell Do You Think You Are," will help you understand how to create your own personal heaven on earth, rather than living in a "hell" of your own creation.

CHERYL LACEY DONOVAN

Motivational Speaker, Talk Show Host, Transformation Expert, National Best Selling Author

A mother and a wife by age 18; abused, separated and a single mom by 20, Cheryl Lacey Donovan knows a little about being unstoppable woman. Despite the obstacles in her way, Cheryl chose to take these life lessons and use them to pave the way to a better future. Cheryl's journey has not been perfect, but it has been blessed. Cheryl chose to look at herself, not in light of what society said she would become, a welfare recipient with children who were drop outs, drug dealers, and in jail, but instead as God viewed her as an awesome, fearfully and wonderfully made virtuous woman. Resilience and tenacity in the face of disappointment helped Cheryl to look inside herself for the change she wanted to see.

Cheryl Lacey Donovan now lives an authentic life as a multi-talented preacher, teacher, mentor, motivational speaker, entrepreneur and author. She is a woman of integrity with a keen level of wisdom and humor that is nothing short of refreshing.

An award winning bestselling author Cheryl has influenced the lives of thousands in the U.S. and abroad through her powerful life changing messages. Desiring to see the saints efficiently armed with the knowledge of God, Cheryl's passion is assisting those in the kingdom, especially women, in discovering their authentic purpose and destiny.

Cheryl's gift of pulling out the very best in those she mentors and pushing them beyond their comfort zone through the word of God has led to her being called a "faith-walker" – calling those things that be not as though they were, she moves in grace and favor. Cheryl is uniquely positioned to impact the lives of individuals she comes in contact with for long term success with her message of faith and powerful vision of bringing purpose into the people equation to promote happier, healthier more meaningful life experiences.

Cheryl presents a powerful message with a conversational style that's just like sitting around chatting with one of your sisters – one who is filled with pearls of wisdom and whose heart is filled with giving. Some of us long for that kind of sister or friend who will just sit you down, tell you the truth about life, share her experiences, and then give you access to a greater more meaningful purpose in life. You will want to sip a warm cup of your favorite drink, bring a note pad and enjoy a candid and educational presentation with Cheryl Lacey Donovan.

ABOUT IMANI FAITH PUBLISHING

Imani Faith Publishing is changing the narrative by telling the stories that need to be told. We are transforming lives, changing mindsets, and writing the words that empower people to empower themselves.

To find out more about Imani Faith Publishing or if you have a story that needs to be told visit our website to learn more about us.

http://www.imanifaithpublishing.com

COMING SOON FROM IMANI FAITH

Imani Faith Publishing is poised to release some of the most prolific works of literature ever written. These stories will do more than entertain. They will empower, inspire, and transform. Readers will be left with an unction to be better and do better.

Early 2016 Imani will release books on stewardship, loss, and abuse. But each of these books will show you how to overcome the tragedy and bask in the triumph.

You won't want to miss any of these powerful heart wrenching and redemptive pieces of literary genius.

Visit Imani Faith Publishing to learn when these books will be available.

http://www.imanifaithpublishing.com

Imani Faith Publishing Presents

OLEVIA HENDERSON

SURVIVING AGAINST ALL ODDS

If You Could See My Scars

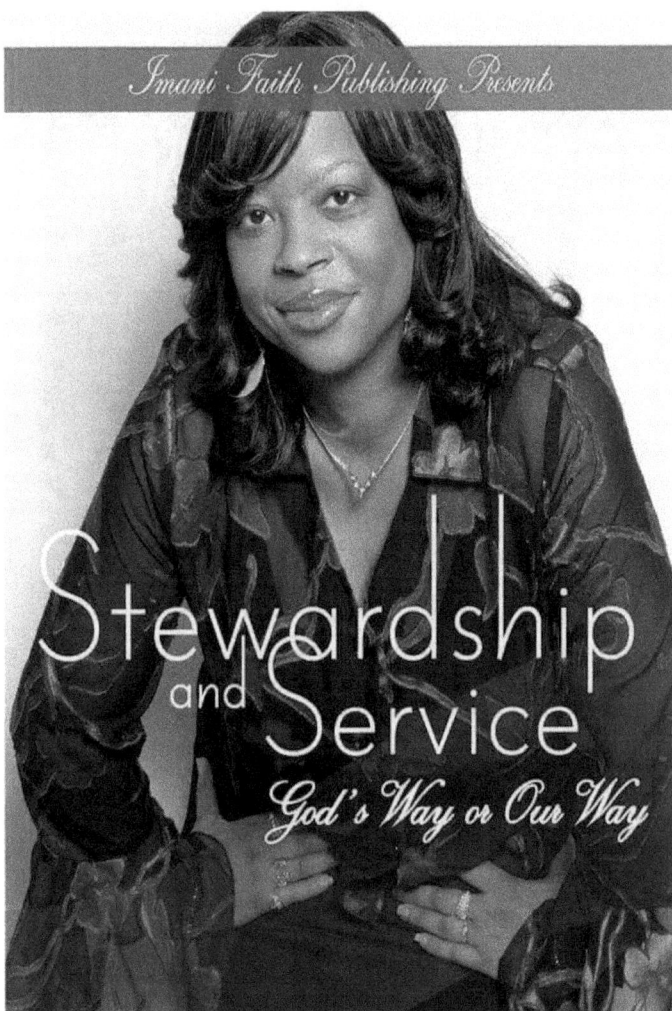

Imani Faith Publishing Presents

Stewardship and Service

God's Way or Our Way

CEE CEE H.
Caldwell-Miller

Imani Faith Publishing Presents

I Was Built for This

MY JOURNEY TO VICTORY

Letisha Galloway